HOW TO PLAY CANASTA

By
RICHARD L. FREY

Introduction by
ELY CULBERTSON

DIVERSEY PUBLISHING CORPORATION
119 West 57th St.   •   New York 19, N. Y.

HOW TO PLAY CANASTA

Copyright, 1949, by Diversey Publishing Corporation

ALL RIGHTS RESERVED
NO PART OF THIS BOOK MAY BE REPRODUCED IN ANY FORM
WITHOUT PERMISSION IN WRITING FROM THE PUBLISHERS

PRINTED IN CANADA

Introduction

For many years Dick Frey was a bridge opponent whose skill I admired and respected. Then, in 1935, I persuaded him to join my team and he became one of my favorite partners. I know how he thinks about games because he has long contributed the fruits of his thinking to the councils of experts who have helped to make the Culbertson system preeminent in bridge.

So before I ever saw this book, I knew it would be a good one. To be great in one card game one must have a deep knowledge of all card games.

Canasta is not a difficult game to play, but it is not an easy game to explain. When you sit down with a deck of cards and start to play, all the "mysteries" of unfamiliar rules become simple. The dozens of actual hands presented in this book bring the written explanation closer to actual play; the presentation of Canasta first as a two-handed game will simplify your learning it.

After reading this book, the beginner may sit down with confidence; the player who has already dabbled in the game will play with increased skill, and even the already skillful player will learn much to add to his strategy. I recommend this book with confidence that all players—beginners and advanced —will be pleased as I am.

ELY CULBERTSON

Contents

INTRODUCTION BY ELY CULBERTSON	3
AUTHOR'S FOREWORD	7
LEARNING CANASTA	9
KEEPING SCORE	24
STRATEGY IN CANASTA—General Principles	30
WHEN TO MAKE THE INITIAL MELD	32
CANASTA FOR TWO	35
Advice on Skillful Play	35
Example Hands	38
CANASTA FOR FOUR	54
Advice on Skillful Play	54
Example Hands	64
LAWS OF CANASTA	105
Players	105
Cards	105
Preliminaries	105
Red Treys	106
Order of Play	107
Melds	107
Canastas	108
Minimum Count	109
Taking the Discard Pile	109
Forcing	111

    Going Out 111
    Scoring a Deal...................................112
    Scoring a Game..................................112
    Concealed Hand 113
IRREGULARITIES 113
    Condonement 113
    New Deal 113
    Deal Out of Turn................................114
    Incorrect Hand 114
    Illegal Draw 115
    Draw Out of Turn................................116
    Insufficient Meld 116
    Illegal Meld 116
    Meld Out of Turn................................117
    Penalty Points 117
    Exposed Cards—Penalty Cards.....................118
    Failure to Declare Red Trey......................118
    Irregularities After Asking Permission to Go Out.....119
    Illegal Looking at Cards.........................119
VARIATIONS IN CANASTA LAWS...................120
CANASTA FOR FIVE............................120
THREE-PACK CANASTA 121
CANASTA FOR SIX.............................121
MATHEMATICS OF CANASTA......................122
GLOSSARY OF CANASTA TERMS...................124

AUTHOR'S FOREWORD

Five years ago my brother returned from a long stay in South America. Shortly after we had greeted each other, he was telling me about a new card game that was becoming immensely popular. I was too smart to listen very carefully; I thought I knew from experience that the American public rarely goes for the kind of game that is popular abroad. I wouldn't even try to play the game with him. Today I couldn't avoid playing it if I wanted to. It was, of course, Canasta.

I don't think it's very important to know that the name "Canasta" comes from a Spanish word for basket. It's more important to know that the best way to win is to pick up the pack when it contains so many cards that you "need a basket" to hold them all in your hand. In Canasta, unlike most other Rummy games, the more cards you can grab the bigger your score will be; the slimmer your hand becomes, the less chance you will have of winning. You will soon see why—but since that is the most important principle of the game, it is well to state it early.

Canasta's American popularity is based on three simple things:

1. Canasta is high-scoring, exciting, subject to such huge swings in the score that it is literally true that you cannot be too far behind to win the game.

2. Canasta is an excellent game for two players, and a good two-handed game is a vital need on far more occasions than even a good four-handed game.

3. Canasta is a perfect four-handed partnership game. Where Gin Rummy played four-handed is, in fact, merely a combination scoring system for two simultaneous two-handed games, Canasta is actually a four-handed game. The partnership fea-

ture lets families play as families, instead of competing against one another. There is no bidding to create arguments, and while the factor of skill is important, the basic theories of skillful play are so easily learned that, with a fair degree of luck, anyone who has played Canasta a few times can beat the most experienced opponents.

I will not attempt to compare Bridge and Canasta. Both are played with cards and there the similarity ends. The great and growing group of people who are crazy about Canasta includes bridge-o-philes and bridge-o-phobes in about equal proportion.

Anyway, why should I try to sell you the game? Canasta is inevitable, you might as well relax and enjoy it.

I am particularly grateful to Ely Culbertson for his introduction to this book because he has written a book of his own (Culbertson on Canasta, published by The John C. Winston Co., Philadelphia).

I am also happy to acknowledge the considerable assistance of Albert H. Morehead and Geoffrey Mott-Smith, and of Sherwin Bash who illustrated the example hands.

But you, the reader, as well as I, the author, are most deeply indebted to John Crawford. He has generously revealed the "secrets" of expert play which account, in part at least, for his virtually unchallenged position as the most skillful Canasta player in America today. And, in spite of the fact that he has held nothing back, you are earnestly cautioned not to challenge Johnny unless you are also able to match his remarkable gifts as one of the world's most expert card players—at bridge or any other game he sits down to play.

RICHARD L. FREY

LEARNING CANASTA

The best way to learn any card game is to listen to the briefest possible explanation of the important rules and then sit down and play it, with someone at your elbow to explain each new feature as it comes up. That is the method followed in this book.

Instead of dealing out the cards, however, you will find the hands already dealt out for you. Thus you will play many deals and meet many situations in a brief time. Then, when you sit down at a table and play in your first real Canasta game, you will already be an experienced player. In fact, you may know more about winning strategy than many people who have played the game for some time.

If you have already played or watched a game of Canasta, you may wish to skip ahead to the end of this chapter and take the "Review Quiz" which covers most of the things you need to know before you are ready to "play" the hands in the following sections.

Canasta is a type of Rummy. Most card players already know Rummy, which is among the easiest of all card games. Nor is Canasta a difficult game to learn. There are, however, so many new features in Canasta that considerable space is required to explain them thoroughly.

In all games of the Rummy family, the object is to match up the cards in your hand to make melding combinations which count points. You do this by drawing a new card at each turn, and discarding one of the cards in your hand; each turn consists of drawing, melding (if you are willing and able to do so), and discarding. The deal ends when one player has melded all his cards, or when the stock is exhausted and the last-discard is of no use to the player who would have the next turn. At the end of the deal the cards you have melded count for you, while the cards which remain in your hand are deducted from your score. There is usually an additional bonus awarded to the player who melds out his entire hand.

How to Play Canasta

All of these rules, with some modification, are a part of the game of Canasta. The first things to learn are the important ways in which Canasta differs from ordinary Rummy. As soon as you know these you can pick up the rest of the game as you play the hands in this book.

The Canasta deck: Canasta is played with a double deck of cards, including four jokers. That makes a pack of 108 cards. All new decks include two jokers, or a joker and an extra card, so any two regular Bridge or Poker decks of the same size may be combined to make a Canasta pack. It does not matter if the two decks are of different back design or different color.

The wild cards: The four jokers and the eight deuces are wild cards to help you make melds.

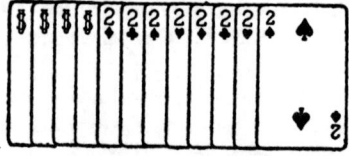

The wild cards

These cards may be used to represent any other card in a meld. However, they may not be melded by themselves. They must be combined with other cards. There can be no meld in Canasta which does not include a natural pair.

These don't count

Learning Canasta   11

These are valid melds

Sequences do not count. You may NOT meld a run like:

THESE DON'T COUNT

The only valid melds are three or more of a kind:

THESE ARE VALID MELDS

Remember, however, that you may use any of the wild **cards to help** you make these melds, except that you must always have **a natural** pair included in each meld. And:

You may not use more than three wild cards in the same meld.

This is O.K.

This is not allowed

Since sequences do not count, suits are of no significance. It does not matter if your meld contains two sevens of hearts or two aces of spades. You do not have to make a meld which includes any special number of cards of different suits.

Threes are special cards. They are not melded like ordinary cards. Whenever you see a three remember that it has a special significance.

Red threes are bonus cards, something like the flowers in a game of Mah Jongg. You never keep a red three in your hand. As soon as you get one (either in the original deal, or by drawing from the deck) you put it face up on the table and draw another card from the stock to replace it in your hand. The draw to replace a red three is an extra draw: it does not count as your regular turn.*

You may not keep a red three concealed (there is a drastic penalty of 500 points if you are caught with one in your hand)

---

* The only time you do not draw to replace a red three is when you pick one up in the discard pile, or when a red three happens to be the last card in the stock. In the latter case the deal ends at once; you face the red three, of course, and may meld, but you are not permitted to discard a card from your hand.

To avoid confusion and possible dispute over who shall have the top-card of the stock, it is customary not to draw to replace red threes dealt to you originally until your first regular turn to play. If someone goes out before your first turn, there is no penalty for having concealed the red three; you simply face it, draw from stock and count the replacement draw as part of the points with which you are caught.

nor is there any reason why you should do so. A red three counts 100 points—200 each if your side has all four of them—and it can never be used as part of a meld, while of course the card you draw to replace it may be of value in making melds.

Threes are special!

Bonus cards. Face them at once and replace with cards drawn from stock.

Black threes may be melded only if you are going out. They are also "stop" cards.

Black threes may not be melded until the turn on which you meld out. On any turn when you can meld all the cards in your hand (or all except the one you intend to discard) you may meld a combination of black threes just like any other meld; you may even use one or more wild cards to help you do so. But you cannot meld black threes until you are going out. Meanwhile, they have a special value as stopcards, for when you discard one your opponent cannot pick it up, not even if it would put him out.

Melding: When a player wishes to make a meld, he puts the cards that form the meld face up on the table. In a partnership game all the melds of one side are kept together, and may be combined.

You may add as many cards as you wish to your own, or to your side's melds. But you may NOT build on an opponent's melds.

In every deal the first player to meld for his side must make a meld which meets certain minimum requirements. You cannot just begin melding any cards that make melds; the first meld for each side in each deal must total a certain amount. This amount varies according to your score.

The value of the melds: The value of each meld is determined solely by the value of the cards melded. Each card has a value in accordance with the following table:

Each joker	50
Each deuce	20
Each ace	20
Each king, queen, jack, ten, nine or eight	10
Each seven, six, five, four or black three	5

These values count for you when melded; they count against you, and are deducted from your score, if you still hold them in your hand when someone goes out, or when the deal ends. In addition to the actual values of the cards, your score is increased by certain bonuses, but these bonuses do not count toward the making of the initial meld.

The minimum melds: When you are starting the game, and until your score has reached 1,500 points, the minimum meld must total at least 50 points. When your score is from 1,500 to 2,995, the minimum initial meld must total at least 90 points. When your score is 3,000 points or more, the initial meld must total at least 120 points. Once a side has made the initial meld there is no longer any minimum requirement; subsequent melds by any player of the side that has made its minimum meld may be as little as a single card added to a previous meld.

The only time there is no minimum requirement for the initial meld is when a side has a "minus" score. If in a previous deal your opponents have gone out and caught you with more points in your hand than you have melded, the net result may be that your score is minus. While your score is in that unhappy condition there is no minimum requirement for your initial meld. It may be only three 5-point cards—15 points—but of course it must be a legal meld in all respects.

Economy in making the minimum meld: While the strategy of the game will be discussed in detail later, it is essential for the Canasta player to realize at the outset the importance of making the minimum meld in the fewest possible cards. You will learn later how the object of the game—making a big score—can best be accomplished; at this point, let it suffice to say that you cannot make a big score without cards in your hand. Thus, while it is desirable to make the minimum meld as early as possible, in most cases it is not desirable to do so at the expense of too greatly reducing the number of cards you will have remaining in your hand.

The examples of initial melds shown on pages 32-34 indicate that you can make the first meld in any way which will make up the total number of points required. At the same time, they point out the desirability of doing so with the expenditure of the fewest possible cards.

Making canastas: The most important meld in the game is a canasta. A canasta is a meld of seven or more cards of the same rank. You may use wild cards to help you make a canasta (but remember you cannot use more than three wild cards in any meld). When you include wild cards, it is called a mixed canasta; when you use only natural cards, it is called a natural canasta. The supreme importance of making canastas is not alone the high bonus it adds to your score; it is this:

You cannot go out until your side has completed one or more canastas. Even if you are able to match up all the cards in your hand, you cannot put the last one down until a canasta has been completed. In two-handed play, the rule is that you must make two canastas before you go out; in four-handed or six-handed play you can go out if anyone on your side has made a canasta. In four-handed or six-handed games you play as a partner of one or two other players, and all your side's melds are counted together. Any partner may add to the melds another partner has made, and a canasta completed by any player on your side,

Natural canasta

Mixed canastas

or by a combination of the melds of all the players on your side, satisfies the rule that you need a canasta in order to go out.

Bonuses: In addition to the actual value of the cards melded, at the end of each deal you are awarded bonuses, as follows:

For each natural canasta (7 or 8 of a kind, no wild cards)	500
For each mixed canasta (7 or more of a kind; one or more wild cards)	300
For going out	100
Going out concealed (player goes out without having previously melded) an additional	100
For each red three	100*
For each red three if all four are held by the same side	200*

*Deducted from your score if your side fails to make any meld.

It is important to remember that red threes are bonus cards, not melds. They do not count toward making a minimum meld. Indeed their value depends upon your being able to make some other meld, for any red threes you have put down will count against you if the deal ends before your side has made any meld. In that case the points they would have scored for you are deducted from your score, in addition to the point value of all the cards which still remain in your hand.

The deal: After the preliminaries which decide the dealer, partners, etc., and after the cards have been shuffled and cut the dealer distributes cards to each player in turn, beginning with the player to his left, one card at a time, until each player has received the proper number of cards. (In two-handed play, each receives 15 cards; in three-handed, each receives 13; with four or more hands each player receives 11.) The remainder of the deck is placed face down in the center of the table and is called the stock. The top card of the stock is then turned and placed face-up alongside the stock. This is called the up-card, and is the foundation of the discard pile.

Stock   Upcard

When upcard is a red three or any wild card, it is covered immediately by another card from stock.

If the dealt up-card happens to be a red three or a wild card, it is covered immediately by another card turned from the top of the stock; as many cards are turned from the stock as necessary, until the up-card is neither a wild card nor a red three.

We are now ready to begin play, but before doing so, you must know under what circumstances you are permitted to take the up-card, and with it all the other cards in the discard pile, in preference to drawing a card from the stock.

Taking the pack: When you are able to use the up-card in an immediate and legal meld, you take all the rest of the discard pile along with it. This is not an optional matter; you *must* take the entire pile. But where this might be a disadvantage in the ordinary Rummy game, in which the sole purpose is to get rid of your cards by melding them as fast as possible, in Canasta taking the pack is a tremendous advantage; in fact, it is the principal strategic object of the game. If you play out a deal by drawing from the stock and discarding one card at every turn, your total melds will have to be made from your original hand. But when you pick up the pack you increase the number of cards with which you can make melds, and give yourself a chance to pile up a big score.

Canasta is a big-score game. You cannot win if you play every hand to go out; you must play to make a big meld, and the only way to do that is by capturing the pack as often as possible. The whole offensive strategy of Canasta is in planning to get the pack; the defensive strategy consists entirely of trying to prevent an opponent from getting it; or, failing that, to go out as quickly as possible.

To make it more difficult to capture the pack, there are certain circumstances in which it is said to be "frozen." (In some games a frozen pack is called a "prize pile".) The pack is frozen whenever it includes a wild card or a red three. It is also frozen to any player whose side has not yet made its initial meld.

When the pack is frozen, you may take it only if you are able to combine the up-card with a natural pair held in your hand. If your side has not yet made its initial meld, you may not take the up-card even with a matching natural pair, unless you are able to meet the minimum meld requirement, using only the up-card in combination with cards already in your hand. (Other cards in the pack may be melded in the same turn, but cannot be counted as part of the initial meld minimum.)

When the pack is not frozen (because you have already made your minimum meld, and because it does not contain a wild card or a red three), you do not need a natural pair; you may take it if you can use the up-card in combination with a matching card and a wild card, or if you can add the up-card to any meld which your side has already made.

As long as there is any stock remaining, you are never compelled to take the up-card. If there are only two or three cards in the discard pile, you may prefer to draw from the stock, though, if there are five or six cards in the discard pile, you will generally prefer to take the pack whenever you can.

When the stock is exhausted, however, you *must* take the up-card if you are able to add it to one of your exposed melds. Sometimes in the end play (when there is nothing of value in the discard pile, or when it is only a single card) you can force your left-hand opponent to pick up your discard, thus giving your partner a chance at his discard. Frequently, this may result in your opponents being forced to make discards which will complete additional canastas for your side. Discarding so as to compel your opponent to pick up the pack is called "forcing."

IMPORTANT: When you take the pack, it is mandatory that you follow this procedure: Do not take any of the cards into your hand; in fact, do not even touch the up-card, until you have put down on the table the cards which you intend to combine with the up-card to make the meld that entitles you to take the pack. This gives the other players opportunity to check the fact that your meld is proper; that it meets the minimum requirement, if it is your initial meld; etc. When you have demonstrated to their satisfaction that you are entitled to take the pack, then you may pick up the remaining cards and put them into your hand. In any case, you always leave the up-card on the table, because that must be combined with an immediate meld.

When the pack has been taken improperly and put into a player's hand, it must be restored to the table; if there is disagreement as to what the pack contained the opponents have the right to examine your hand, if necessary, in order to determine what cards should be restored. You will avoid errors and disputes if you observe the proper procedure for taking the pack, as outlined above.

Stop-cards: You may not pick up the pack if the up-card is a wild card or a black three. These cards are called stop-cards. The effect of discarding a wild card is also to freeze the pack, if it is not already frozen. However, a black three, though it prevents the next player from taking the pack, does not freeze it. A red three is not a stop card, because it may never be discarded. The only way it can get into the pack is if it is the first card the dealer turns, and in that case it is immediately covered by another card from the stock.

Stop-cards

Going out: You may go out whenever your side has completed the necessary canasta(s) and whenever you are able to meld all the cards in your hand, except the one you will discard. (It is not necessary for you to discard, however; if you can meld all your cards, you may do so.) In a partnership game, however, you are accorded the privilege of consulting your partner, provided you do so before making any meld on that turn. Before or after you have drawn, but before you have melded, you say "May I go out partner?" If he says yes, you must do so; if he says no, you may not do so on that turn. (In a six-handed game, where you have two partners, you may address your question to either one, but only he may answer.) You must be careful about the procedure of asking this question, however. There are penalties if you should ask and then find you are unable to go out; there is also a penalty if you ask when you have already made some meld on that turn.

This means that you may not take the up-card and then ask, for to take the up-card you must meld. But you may ask before drawing at all, and then, after your partner answers, you may take the pack if you wish.

You may go out without asking your partner's permission, if you wish. In most cases, however, it is an advantage to be able to ask his advice.

When you have only one card remaining in your hand you may not go out by picking up a discard pile consisting of only one card, provided you can draw from the stock. This applies only to the specific situation where you hold one card in your hand, the up-card is the only one in the discard pile, and there is at least one card left in the stock. You may pick up a discard pile of two or more cards, though you have only one card in your hand, and you may also pick up a discard pile of only one card if you have two or more cards in your hand.

When a player reduces his hand to only one card, it is proper for him to announce that fact at once. At any time during the game the player whose turn it is may ask how many cards remain in the hands of the other players. This is a privilege which may be of considerable value in deciding whether to go out, and whether to ask partner for permission to go out.

A player in turn may also count the cards remaining in the stock; but it is never permissible to look back at previous discards.

Going out "Concealed": There is a special bonus of 100 points for going out "concealed." It is earned by a player who melds out his entire hand in one turn, without having made any previous meld. But even when a player goes out in one turn he does not earn the bonus if he adds any cards to his partner's melds, or, if his melds do not include a complete canasta of his own. (His side must have a canasta in any case, of course, but a canasta made by partner does not qualify to earn the "concealed" bonus.)

There are really only two advantages to playing to go out concealed. One is the possibility of catching the opponents early with big scores still in their hands; the other is that when a player goes out concealed he does not need to meet any specific minimum meld requirement. Even if his side would normally need 120 points as a minimum, he can go out with any point count provided his hand meets all the other requirements.

Under all other circumstances there is no advantage to playing to go out concealed; surely the 100-point bonus is so insignificant compared with other Canasta bonuses that it should hardly be considered.

Procedure during the play: One player on each side keeps the melds in front of him; it is the other's job to keep the score. To conserve table space, it is customary to close the fan of a meld into a pile when a canasta has been completed. A black card on top marks a mixed canasta; a red card marks a natural canasta and warns you not to add a wild card to it.

The red three or wild card which freezes the pack is usually placed at the bottom of the discard pile crosswise to the rest of the pile so that the projecting card is a reminder that the pack is frozen.

Scoring: In a partnership game, it is customary for one partner of each side to check the count of the opponents' melds. A canasta score can run very large and when two people add it is usually more accurate.

The bonuses are usually counted first, because they can be counted before disturbing the piles which mark completed canastas, etc. Thereafter the point values of the cards are counted. Most canasta scorepads have two lines for the scoring of each deal; the bonus score and the point value of the cards are entered separately; then added to the previous score. The final total is announced at the beginning of the next deal to remind each player of the required minimum for his initial meld. (In counting the basic value of the melds, cast aside red threes as soon as the bonus scores have been entered. Red threes have no value except their bonus value.)

In most games it is customary to figure the final score of each side, at the end of the game, to the nearest 100; in this case a score of 50 or more counts as 100, and anything less than 50 is not counted. However, a side must actually pass the 5,000 point before the game ends; if at the end of a hand the score is 4,970 to 4,300, the game continues.

The game ends at the conclusion of the deal where one score is 5,000 points or more. If more than one score is over 5,000 it does not matter. There is no bonus for winning the game. The winners enter the net difference in scores on a separate tally. There is no carry-over of score from game to game. If there is a tie at 5,000 points or more the game ends as a tie; there is no play-off.

See the scoring illustrations on pages 24 and 25.

The CANASTA SCORE provides two separate lines for entering the totals made by each side on each deal. The first line is used for the bonus scores; the second line for the value of the card points melded, less the value of the cards which remain in the hands. The next line records the total score with which each side begins the next deal. This total governs the initial meld requirements for the next deal.

PLAYERS	CANASTA SCORE	
	(A-B)	(C-D)
	WE	THEY
Bonuses	−200	400
Card Points	−195	220
TOTAL	−395	620
Bonuses	500	700
Card Points	190	245
TOTAL	295	1565
Bonuses	400	1100
Card Points	195	340
TOTAL	890	3005
Bonuses	2000	
Card Points	475	155
TOTAL	3365	3160
Bonuses	1500	800
Card Points	465	210
TOTAL	5330	4170

1st deal: (Each side needs 50.) THEY went out before WE melded, catching us with two red threes and 195 points in cards. THEY got one mixed canasta (300), for going out 100, and in card points THEY scored 220.

2nd deal: (THEY need 50, WE can make any initial meld, even as little as 15, because we start with a minus score.) THEY go out with two mixed canastas. WE have one mixed canasta and two red threes.

3rd deal: (WE need 50; THEY need 90.) Again THEY go out. THEY had three mixed canastas; 100 for a red three; 100 for going out. WE had a mixed canasta and a red three.

4th deal: (WE need 50; THEY need 120.) WE get them in a squeeze and score one natural and four mixed canastas (1,700), two red threes (200), for going out (100). THEY had no bonuses since they made no canasta and had no red threes; THEY melded a net 155 in cards.

5th deal: (Both sides need 120.) WE go out with one natural canasta and three mixed canastas. THEY make two mixed canastas and also held two red threes.

WE have over 5,000 points and win the game. Our net score, 5,330, is reduced for convenience to the nearest 100, or 5,300. Their net score is figured as 4,200. Our net gain is 1,100 points, scored on a separate tally, on which A and B appear individually as plus 11, B and C are individually minus 11.

Additional information: There are a few other points which have not been specifically covered in this basic outline of the mechanics of play. They are situations which come up infrequently, and are covered by the official rules (see pages 000). Most of these are situations where the rules have been violated and the question is a matter of penalty, or of correcting the error. Others are the result of interpreting laws which apply to other games so that they will be suited to Canasta.

For example, while a player may combine any of his side's melds, he may not split a meld. No card may be withdrawn from a meld once it has been placed on the table. This includes the joker; in Canasta, there is no privilege of substituting a natural card for the joker as there is, for example, in Oklahoma. There is no extra bonus for building a canasta larger than seven cards; on the other hand, there is no rule which prohibits you from adding as many cards as you wish to any meld—except for the rule that not more than three wild cards may be included in the same meld. Even this rule is suspended as regards adding wild cards to a canasta that has already been completed.

In any game as new as Canasta there are bound to be many innovations played as "local options" which are not part of the official rules. Some of these optional rules are listed on page 000. But at least until you have played the game for some little time, it is recommended that you follow the rules exactly as set forth in the official laws, including the penalties. Many players do not like to exact penalties in a friendly game, yet the penalties are not imposed to inflict punishment but rather to correct any injustice which an innocent breach of the laws may have caused the non-offending side.

REVIEW QUIZ

If you can answer these questions, you are ready to play the hands which follow.

1. How much do sequences count?
2. How many cards are there in the Canasta pack? How many of these are wild cards?
3. What is the maximum number of wild cards you may use in a single meld?
4. When can you make a meld that does not include a natural pair?
5. What is a natural canasta? A mixed canasta?
6. How many canastas do you need before you can go out?
7. When is the pack "frozen"?
8. What is the point value of a meld of Joker-Ace-deuce?
9. When can you pick up the discard of a black three?
10. What is the minimum meld required if your score is minus? If it's 0-1,495? 1,500-2,995? 3,000 or more?
11. Which cards in the discard pile can you use in making a minimum initial meld?
12. Can you go out without asking your partner's permission?
13. Can you go out if your side has not made a canasta?
14. Can you go out without discarding?
15. If you have not made a minimum meld yourself, can you add cards to your partner's melds?
16. What happens when you draw a red three?
17. How much are red threes worth? If your side has all four? If your side has not made any meld?
18. What happens when you discard a red three?
19. When can you take the up-card without taking the rest of the discard pile?
20. When the pack is frozen, what do you need to take it?
21. What do you need when the pack is not frozen?

22. How many points do you need for game?

23. If you start a deal with a score of 4,880 points, when you make your minimum meld of 120 points, is the game over?

24. Does a natural canasta of fours satisfy the requirement for a minimum meld?

25. Can you ever meld black threes? If so, when?

26. What happens if there are no cards left in the stock pile?

27. What is the penalty if you are caught with a red three in your hand?

28. What is the procedure if the dealt up-card is a red three? A wild card? A black three?

29. Do a red three and a 30-point meld make a 120-point minimum meld?

30. Can you add cards to a completed canasta?

ANSWERS

1. Nothing: you cannot meld sequences.
2. 108; 12, eight deuces and four jokers.
3. Three.
4. You can't.
5. Seven matched cards, no wild cards; a mixed canasta contains one or more wild cards.
6. One in partnership play; two if the game is two-handed.
7. When it contains a wild card or red three, also whenever your side has not yet made its initial meld.
8. Nothing; you may not make a meld which does not include a natural pair.
9. Never, it is a stop-card.
10. Any meld; 50, 90, 120.
11. Only the up-card.
12. Yes.
13. No.
14. Yes.

15. Yes.
16. You face it on the table and draw another card from stock.
17. 100, 200; they are deducted from your score.
18. You may not do so.
19. Never.
20. A natural pair to match the up-card.
21. A matching card and a wild card; or you may add the up-card to a meld you have already made.
22. 5,000.
23. No; once started, a deal must be played out.
24. No; only the point value of the cards counts towards the minimum initial meld. Bonus values are not counted, unless you can go out "concealed."
25. Yes, on the turn in which you go out.
26. If the next player cannot use the last discard, the deal ends.
27. 500 points, provided you have had at least one turn to play.
28. It is covered with the top card of the stock if it is a wild card or a red three; if it is a black three, the first player must draw from stock.
29. No. Red threes are bonus cards, they do not count as melds.
30. Yes; including any number of wild cards.

GENERAL STRATEGY

Canasta is a high-scoring game; in order to win at it, you need 5,000 points; therefore, you must play to meld big. You cannot win by following the strategy of Gin-rummy, for example, and trying to match up your hand and meld out as fast as possible. You might succeed in melding out on every deal and still find yourself far behind.

Obviously, you cannot get a very big meld from the number of cards dealt to you originally. The only way to meld big is to get the pack; your primary object, therefore, is to capture the pack, and to prevent your opponents from taking it.

To have the best chance of taking the pack yourself, as well as to play defensively so that your opponents cannot take it, you need to keep as many cards as possible in your hand. Therefore, we may state some fundamental principles to which there are few exceptions:

1. Make your initial meld with the fewest possible cards.
2. Take the pack whenever doing so will return to your hand as many cards, or more cards than you must meld in order to take it.
3. Do not be in too great a hurry to make any meld which will deplete your hand.
4. When the pack is building up to substantial proportions, if you cannot take it yourself it is worth some sacrifice to discard a card which will insure that the enemy cannot take it.
5. If you have a hand which includes several cards that are potentially dangerous discards, try to get rid of some of the dangerous cards while the pack is small when it will be less costly if the opponents are able to pick it up.

It may seem, on the face of it, dangerous to keep building up your hand whenever you can. Under the rules, if an opponent goes out the point values of all the cards in your hand are deducted from your score. However, if you will refer to the scoring table, you cannot fail to observe that the point value of the cards is so much less than the point value of canastas as to become almost insignificant.

The total point value of the entire Canasta pack, excluding the bonus values of the red threes, is only 1,180. Of course, you could not possibly have all these points because your opponents must have some cards. But if you can keep the opponents from getting the pack, and from going out, it is possible to score more than 5,000 points on a single deal. If, for example, you were able to make five natural canastas, the bonus value would total 2,500 points alone.

In playing to get the pack, it would seem that the low cards must be of as great value as the high cards, and that it would be just as sound to throw high cards early as it is to throw low ones. The necessity for making a minimum number of points in your initial meld is the principal reason why this is not true. In order to make the initial meld with the fewest possible cards it is necessary to meld high cards; and as the initial minimum rises to 90 and then 120 the high cards become even more important. That is why the early discards tend to be low cards. Usually by the time you have made your minimum meld both you and your opponents have discarded several ranks of low cards, and you are both grimly saving high cards.

Even when you have taken a substantial pack, therefore, the principle of melding as few cards as possible continues. The melds you hold in your hand are as good, for taking the pack again, as pairs held in your hand. Put them on the table, however, and if the opponents freeze the pack they can in relative safety discard the cards that match your melds. However when you can make a meld and still retain a pair of the same rank in your hand it is usually desirable to do so. An exception may occur when you foresee the possible need to reserve all the cards of this rank as safe future discards.

These are only the broad outlines of Canasta strategy. Specific strategy for the two-handed game is discussed beginning on page 35; for partnership play, beginning on page 54.

INITIAL MELDS: Minimum at 50.

Best possible because minimum is made by melding only 3 cards.

Good; even though requiring four cards to make 50 points.  or

  55 points; a proper initial meld, but not a very good one because it takes six cards.

Only 35 points; therefore not a valid meld in spite of being a natural canasta. You may count only the point value of the cards; bonus values don't count.

50 points. O.K. However, this has taken so many of your cards it is a plea for partner to help you go out fast.

INITIAL MELDS: Minimum at 90

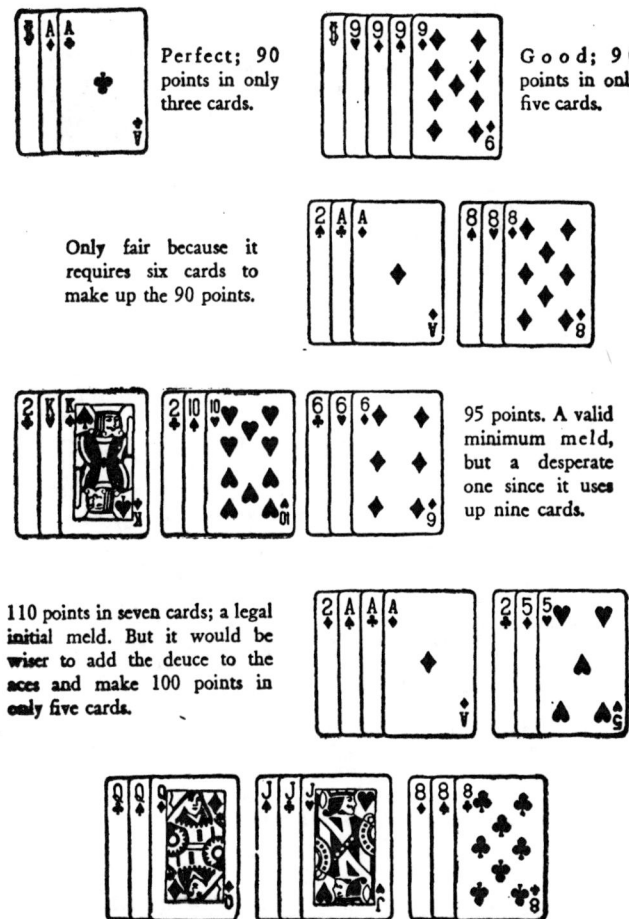

Perfect; 90 points in only three cards.

Good; 90 points in only five cards.

Only fair because it requires six cards to make up the 90 points.

95 points. A valid minimum meld, but a desperate one since it uses up nine cards.

110 points in seven cards; a legal initial meld. But it would be wiser to add the deuce to the aces and make 100 points in only five cards.

90 points in nine cards. Valid, but a desperate meld unless you have taken a substantial pile by the play which made this meld.

INITIAL MELDS: Minimum at 120

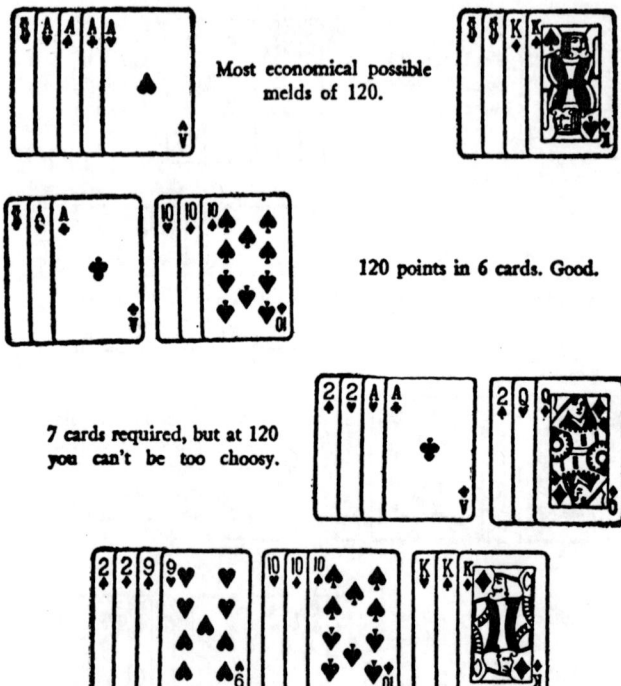

Most economical possible melds of 120.

120 points in 6 cards. Good.

7 cards required, but at 120 you can't be too choosy.

10 cards—a desperation minimum. Better wait to improve your 10s or kings or get another wild card, and concentrate the meld into two ranks. However, if you must meld, add one of the deuces to the tens or kings. You don't worry about making natural canastas when you are in such straits.

Note: When the minimum is at 120 it is sometimes advisable for one partner to wreck his hand, if necessary, in order to get down. Without at least one joker, or aces and deuces, you can't make 120 economically.

CANASTA FOR TWO

Most people who are learning Canasta begin by playing two-handed with someone who already knows the game. Although there are quite a few strategic differences between two-hand (or three-hand) and partnership play, a two-handed game is a good way to start. It is also a good game to play—for it is probably true that at present the majority of Canasta games around the country are played two-handed, despite the fact that practically all club play is the four-handed partnership game.

Primarily, the strategy of two-handed play is defensive. The first player to get a substantial pack has an enormous advantage and can frequently continue to keep getting the pack for as long as that deal lasts. The requirement that a player must complete two canastas makes it almost impossible to go out concealed (not that you'd really want to) and very difficult for a player to stave off disaster by playing to go out fast.

It is absolutely essential to try to make a big score on every deal. When you are fortunate enough to control the pack you should play to make a killing score; defer going out until you have wrung the last possible meld out of that deal. You will need everything you can get if the luck changes and your opponent controls the pack on the next deal.

Playing to take the pack means keeping as many cards as possible in your hand; melding as few cards as necessary until you are able to meld and still retain pairs of the same rank so that your opponent cannot ever safely discard that rank even if the pack is frozen.

It is suicidal to deplete your hand to any appreciable extent, even to meld initially: The advantage of making the initial meld early is not particularly great. You have no partner to assist, or to give you assistance, and unfreezing the pack may be so brief an advantage that it is not worth sacrificing cards.

In general, therefore, you should never make the initial meld until you are forced to do so in order to take the pack; even then, you may decline to do so unless the pack will restore to your hand the number of cards you must give up to make the meld, or, rarely, if it will not quite do so but it will relieve an immediate discarding problem.

Possible exceptions to this rule of never depleting your hand to make the initial meld are:

1. A meld of three aces, which is so economical that it may be worthwhile, since it will force your opponent to toss a wild card or to make an initial meld to put himself on an equal footing with you. Or, with an initial requirement of 90, a meld of two aces and a joker may also be considered. The reason: You can never make an initial meld more cheaply and you will not, in any case, wish to discard your aces, nor is your opponent likely to do so. Since those places in your hand will be permanently occupied by the aces anyway, you are not really sacrificing places when you meld them.

2. Late in the game, when the opponent has grabbed the pack and seems destined to make a big score anyway, you might as well make some meld and save what you can from the wreckage.

What is in the pack is rarely of any importance; the only thing that is important is how many cards it contains. When you take up a pack of "useless" cards (useless as far as melds are concerned) they are nevertheless useful in providing discards. And actually safe discards are the most useful things you can have in two-hand play.

In the early play, you choose your discards for safety, at the same time trying to build your own hand so that:

(a) You are able to make the minimum meld whenever you wish to.

(b) You have the greatest possible number of pairs with which to take the pack. (Pairs are more important than triplets. The third card in the triplet is unnecessary to help you take the pack and it crowds out another and perhaps more useful card.

Canasta for Two

This is particularly true of low cards, with which, in any case, you could not afford to make the initial meld except in the course of taking a substantial pack.)

In the later play, and particularly when the pack has built up, you must often disregard your own hand in the greater interests of safety. In other words, two-handed Canasta is a game of "safety first" in discards. And last. And practically always.* Only in the very early plays, when there are practically no cards in the discard pile, can you afford a risky discard.

The result, as a rule, is that sooner or later your wild cards become your only safe discards. Eventually one player or the other makes a bad guess, or gets into a squeeze where any card he throws will give his opponent the pack. When that happens, the unfortunate player who yields is at the mercy of his opponent—and Canasta is a merciless game. As you will soon see.

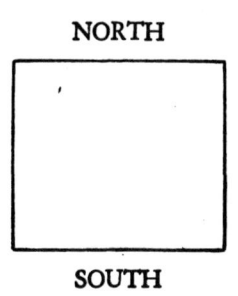

NORTH

SOUTH

In all the following example hands, YOU are South.

---

*However, there is no sense butting your head against a stone wall. Once the opponents control the pack you will have to give, and give, and give. If you can foresee the inevitability of this, you may as well save your wild cards and melds and play to go out at whatever cost.

HAND 1.

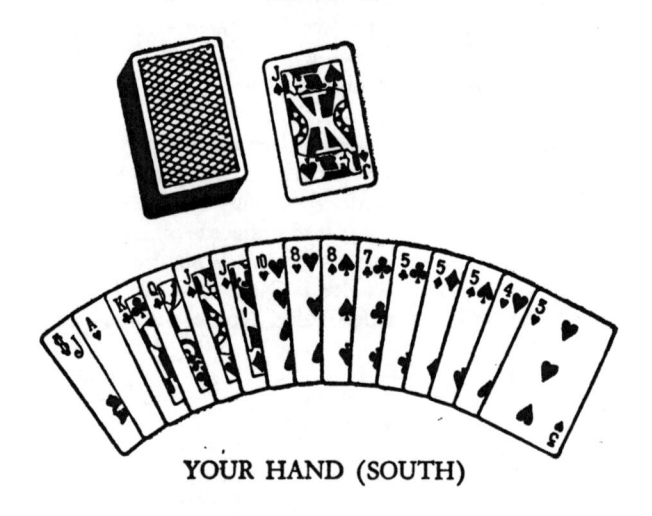

YOUR HAND (SOUTH)

North deals. Both sides need 50.

QUESTION: (a) What do you do first?

ANSWER: Put your red trey face up on the table and draw a replacement card from the stock. You draw a deuce. Now:

QUESTION: (b) What do you do next?

ANSWER: Decide whether you will take the up-card or draw from the stock. In this hand you can do either because you have a natural pair of jacks in your hand and adding your joker will more than make the minimum meld. However, with only one card in the discard pile it is best to draw from the stock. The important point to remember is that the draw to replace your red three(s) is in addition to your regular draw.

HAND 2.

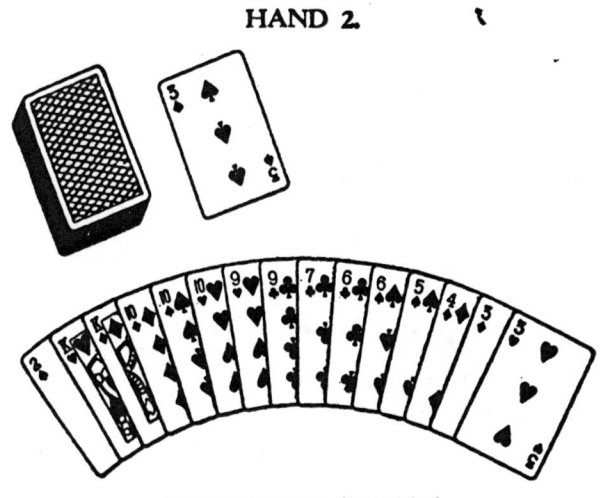

YOUR HAND (SOUTH)

You deal. Both sides need 50.

QUESTION: (a) What do you do about the black three?

(b) What do you about your red treys?

ANSWER: (a) Nothing. Your opponent may not take it, because it is a stop-card. However, it is not necessary to cover it with another card drawn from stock, as it would be if the dealt up-card were a red three or a wild card.

(b) Wait until North has completed his first turn; then place your two red treys face up on the table, draw two replacements from the stock, and then decide whether to continue by taking his discard (if you can—and in which case you would also take up the black trey under it) or drawing a third card from stock as your regular turn. With only two cards in the discard pile it is almost certain you will wish to draw from stock.

HAND 3.

YOUR HAND (SOUTH)

North deals. Both sides need 50.

QUESTION: Can you take the up-card so as to meld K-K-K?

ANSWER: No, because the value of this meld is only **30**. For the initial meld of a deal you must meet a certain minimum requirement, which is never less than 50 unless you start the deal with a minus score. You could not meet this minimum even by melding your sevens along with the kings, for the three sevens count only 15. Anyway, you wouldn't want to make this meld even if you could; it would take too many cards out of your hand.

HAND 4.

YOUR HAND (SOUTH)

You deal. Both sides need 50. North draws, then discards an eight. Now there are an eight and a ten in the pack.

QUESTION: Can you take the pack in order to meld 8-8-8 and 10-10-10?

ANSWER: No. You must always meet the required minimum (in this case, 50) using only cards already in your hand plus only the top card of the pack. You may not use any of the other cards in the pack to make up your initial minimum. If you can legally take the pack, you may meld any or all the cards you find in it, but only after you have made the minimum meld.

HAND 5.

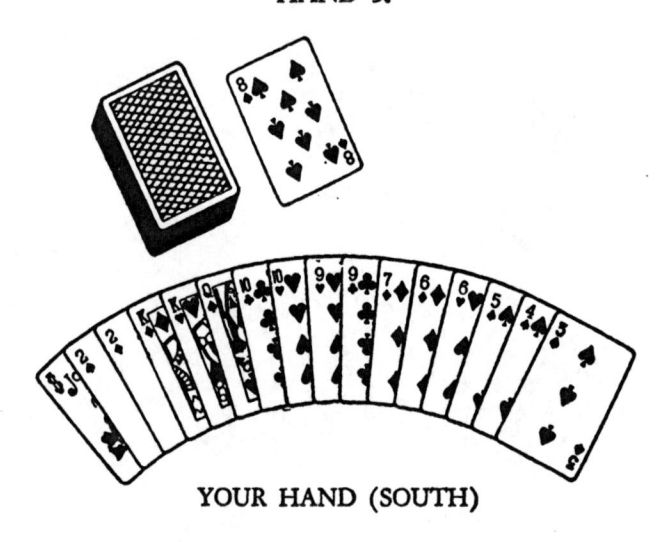

YOUR HAND (SOUTH)

North deals. Both sides need 50. You have just drawn a ten from the stock.

QUESTION: Should you make an initial meld?

ANSWER: No. All that you do thereby is to unfreeze the pack for yourself. As soon as North feels he has no safe discard he will freeze it again by discarding a wild card. The net result is that you have relinquished a pair in your hand with which you might otherwise have taken the pack. Once you meld, e. g., your pair of kings, your opponent can throw kings so long as the pack is frozen. Paste this in your hat: At the two-handed game, the correct policy (except for a few situations) is to meld just as little as you are obliged to, until you choose to go out. Postpone the initial meld until taking the pack requires you to make one.

HAND 6.

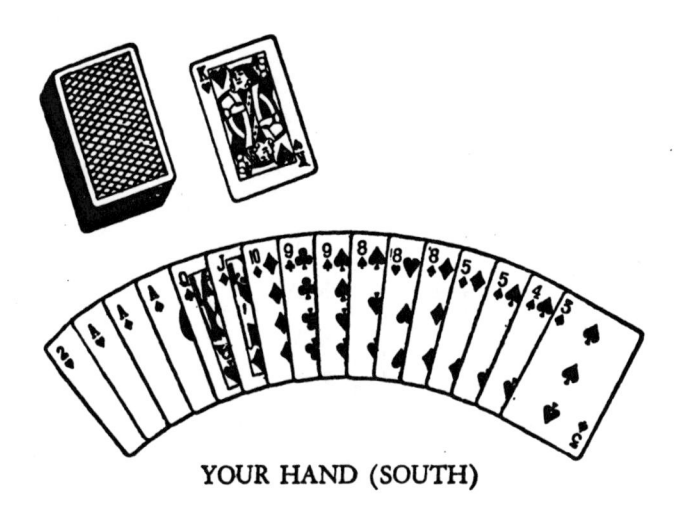

YOUR HAND (SOUTH)

North deals. Both sides need 50. You have just drawn the queen from the stock.

QUESTION: Should you make an initial meld of A-A-A?

ANSWER: Yes. One of the exceptions to the rule given in Hand 5 concerns aces. Neither of you will discard an ace (counting 20) unless you see that the play is absolutely safe. Hence you have nothing to gain by concealing your trio of aces.

The three-card meld is the most economical possible. Make it at once so as to get a tactical edge. The pack is now unfrozen to you. North will be under compulsion to equalize the situation, either by making an initial meld to unfreeze the pack for himself, or tosing a wild card to freeze it for you. Either way you may make difficulty for him.

HAND 7.

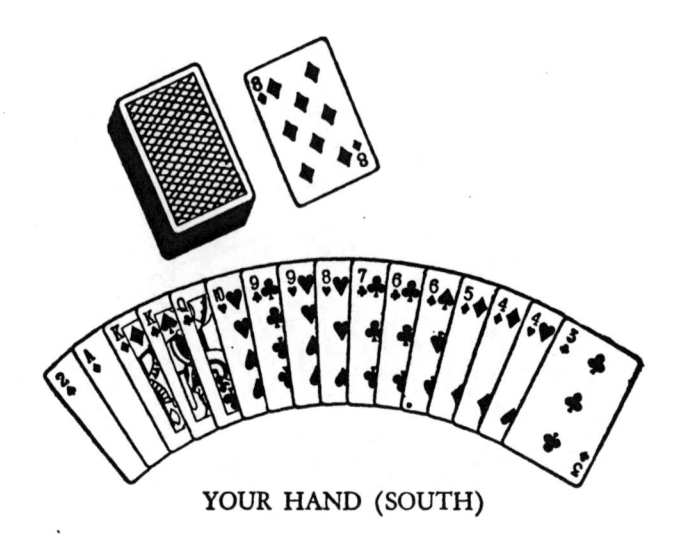

YOUR HAND (SOUTH)

North dealt. Both sides need 50. You could **not** take the upcard and drew from the stock.

QUESTION: What should you discard?

ANSWER: Your unmatched seven or five. This is one of the few cases in which you hold onto a black three rather than discard it. Black threes are unusable cards and fill up space that might better be used for live cards. But on your next play you must throw something other than a three anyway. You may as well throw it now, when the pack is so small your opponent won't bother to take it. When there are more cards in the pack, it will be time enough to use the black trey.

HAND 8.

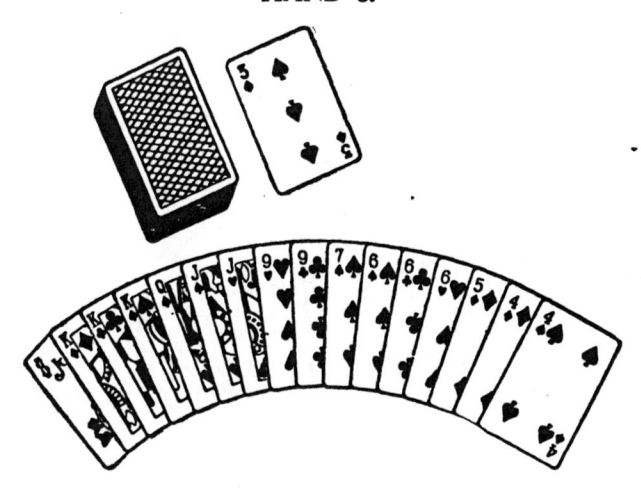

YOUR HAND (SOUTH)

North deals. Both sides need 50. You have just drawn a five from the stock.

QUESTION: What should you discard?

ANSWER: A six. You certainly will never want to deplete your hand by melding the sixes. You will meld low cards (counting 5 each) from the pack, but not from your hand. The utility of low cards in your hand is to snare the pack. For this purpose, a pair is better than a trio, because it does not take up so much room. If dealt a low trio, discard one early—both as "bait," to convey the impression to your opponent that he can discard this rank with safety, and to make room in your hand for a card of another rank.

HAND 9.

YOUR HAND (SOUTH)

North deals. Both sides need 50.

QUESTION: Should you take the up-card to make an initial meld of Q-Q-Q and 9-9-9?

ANSWER: No. Leave the queen as a kind of "advertising," next-best to a voluntary discard from a trio (see Hand 8). In the two-handed game, it does not pay to make an initial meld from your hand alone with anything but aces. In other words, aim to make your initial meld (a) with the minimum number of cards from hand alone, or (b) in taking the pack. To expend six cards to make a mere 50 is not a good investment.

HAND 10.

YOUR HAND (SOUTH)

You deal. Both sides need 50. North, after drawing, discards: (a) a black three. (b) a four.

QUESTION: (a) Should you take the pack to meld Joker-3-3-3?

(b) Should you take the pack to meld Joker-4-4-4?

ANSWER: (a) No. You may never take a black three; it is a stopcard.

(b) No. Why take the pack now, when it is so small? Your prospect of getting it later, when it contains more booty, is excellent. You can afford to save low pairs, which always have a better chance of matching the top card of the pack than do high cards, because your joker will always enable you to make a count of 50. And you have no immediate concern about discarding since you have a couple of black threes available for that purpose.

HAND 11.

IN THE PACK:
7-3-3-3-7

YOUR HAND (SOUTH)

You dealt. Both sides need 50. The up-card is North's third discard. The pack is as shown.

QUESTION: Should you take the pack?

ANSWER: Yes. Take it and meld 9-9-9-2. The most important consideration in taking the pack very early is whether doing so will deplete your hand. Here you can pick up six cards, meld four, discard one, making a net gain of one card.

Another vital reason for taking the pack is to get those black treys. This may seem a paradox in view of what was said under Hand 5. You will, of course, hasten to discard the black treys, but you have gained three perfectly safe discards at the very time when picking a safe discard is most difficult—the beginning of the game. The treys do not displace usable cards, in the sense stated under Hand 5. They displace your nines, which you would not want to discard anyhow. By taking the pack, you still have your nines, plus three additional spaces to hold usable cards. Your opponent will be unable to throw a nine unless he freezes the pack.

The sevens you get in the pack are added riches. So long as you have this pair, North is barred from discarding a seven at any time the pack is worth taking. Of course he knows it—but what can he do about it? There is one less rank he can discard safely.

How to Play Canasta

HAND 12.

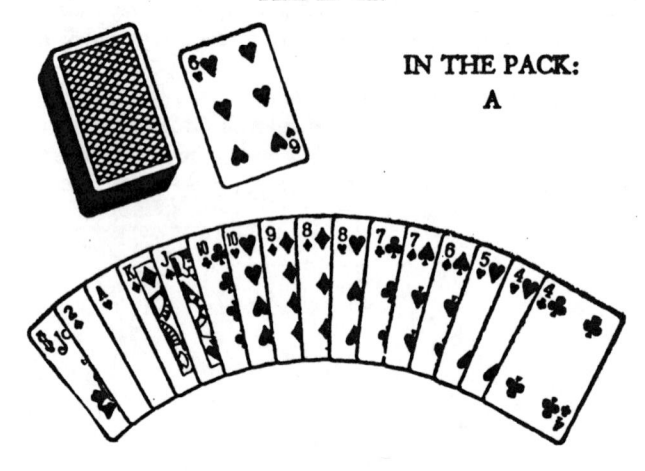

IN THE PACK:
A

YOUR HAND (SOUTH)

You dealt. Both sides need 50. You have just drawn from the stock.

QUESTION: What should you discard?

ANSWER: A six. The safest discards at the very beginning of the game are the same ranks your opponent discards. If he is simply ridding his hand of odd cards, then your discards won't "hit" him. But suppose he is "advertising" by discarding from a trio, as in Hand 6? Your best defense is (usually) to get rid of your "feeders" while the pack is young. Then, as in this case, if he takes the pack he will have to deplete his hand to make the initial meld. If you keep your six in the belief that he still has a pair, it will become an embarrassment that snowballs as the pack grows larger. Even if you were absolutely certain he held a pair of sixes you should throw your six at once.

Canasta for Two 51

HAND 13.

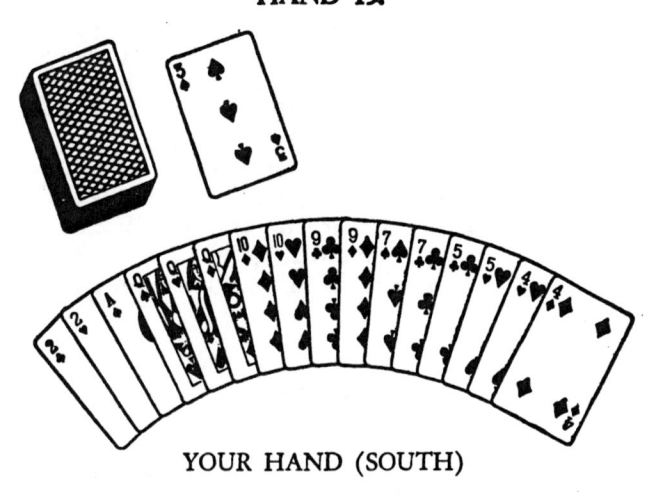

YOUR HAND (SOUTH)

You dealt. Both sides need 50. North has taken the up-card to meld A-A-A. You have drawn a five.

QUESTION: Should you meld? In either case, what should you discard?

ANSWER: North has unfrozen the pack for himself and can now take it with one natural and one wild card, or if you discard any card which will match a meld he has already made. You still need a natural pair to take it. Sooner or later you must restore equality.

One way is to make an initial meld yourself, say Q-Q-Q-2, thus unfreezing the pack for you too. But that is a bad way, particularly with this hand. Depleting your hand, except under direst necessity or for huge gain, is poor business.

The other way to gain equality is to discard a deuce, freezing the pack for both you and your opponent. This is by far the better way, especially when you hold a number of natural pairs.

52   *How to Play Canasta*

You not only save all fifteen cards in your hand, but you also provide for the future. If the pack grows to any size you will find it increasingly difficult to make safe discards—probably impossible if North is free to take the pack with only one natural card. Your chance of saving the pack from his predatory paw is much better if he needs a natural pair.

The beginner at Canasta is too prone to worry about risking a wild card in a pack which his opponent may pick up. Your entire strategy must be built around planning to pick up the pack yourself; if your opponent is going to be able to continue picking it up, another wild card in your hand will not save you from disaster.

HAND 14.

IN THE PACK:
J-3

YOUR HAND (SOUTH)

North dealt. Both sides need 50. You have just made your second draw, a six.

QUESTION: (a) Should you meld, and, if so, what?
(b) What should you discard?

ANSWER: (a) No. You could meld kings or sevens with the joker, but why deplete your hand? (If the situation were such that you did choose to meld, the kings—two of them, not three—with the joker are better than the sevens because the sevens represent a better early prospect for getting the pack.)

(b) Let go a deuce. You can't meld wild cards alone: you need natural pairs to make wild cards of any use. In this hand, all your other cards are more valuable than the deuces.

After you have played a few times, you will see many late-stage situations where wild cards are trash, natural cards worth their weight in gold. It will seem less unnatural to discard wild cards. Of course, not often are you dealt a hand with more wild cards than you can use, as in this case; still, it does happen. Don't get the fixed idea that the only purpose in throwing a deuce is to freeze the pack.

CANASTA FOR FOUR

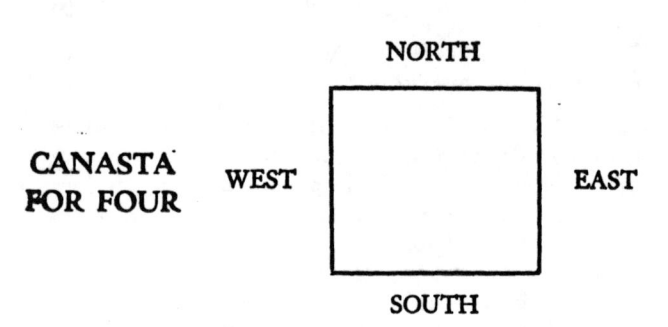

```
        NORTH
    ┌─────────┐
WEST│         │EAST
    │         │
    └─────────┘
        SOUTH
```

The constants of Canasta strategy—the struggle for control of the pack, and the play to keep as many cards as possible in your hand—remain unchanged in partnership play. But many other elements are altered radically.

No longer can you consider only what is best for your own hand. You must play as a team, just as you meld as a team. Strangers to the technique of four-handed play usually make two mistakes. At first they fail to consider what partner may be up against, or be trying to do. Then the pendulum swings too far the other way and they cripple their own hands in an effort to help good old partner. Neither policy will succeed. One of the greatest elements of skill in the four-handed game is the exercise of good judgment in helping your partner at the same time you help yourself.

While you acquire a partner, you also acquire another opponent. Aside from the fact that you now have two people who are trying to beat you, the mechanics of the game have changed; you get only one play in four instead of every other turn. This has two immediate effects: Your "dangerous" discard is not so certain to be dangerous. The player to your left may not be the one who is saving that rank; your partner and your right-hand opponent may have it. By the same token, the cards of the ranks you could use may be discarded by your left-hand opponent and your partner without helping you in the slightest.

In addition to remembering what is in the discard pile, you must now remember who put what cards there. The mere fact that it includes a couple of sixes may mean nothing if your left-hand opponent has not thrown either of them—that is, nothing beyond the mathematical fact that the more cards of any rank have been thrown, the less is the chance that any player still holds a natural pair of that rank.

However, this does not mean that you can be content to keep track of the cards your left-hand opponent has discarded, or has failed to discard, and forget about the discards of the other players. Your partner's discards will tell you what ranks he is probably holding, and whether or not he seems to be in trouble. Your right-hand opponent's discards will tell you what you are most likely to get in his future discards to you. As the game progresses, a skillful player can make fairly shrewd guesses about the kind of hand each of the other players has.

One of the points few but the most expert players realize is that, in the early play, you will do well to copy the discards of your *right*-hand opponent—the player who is discarding to you. If this seems odd advice, consider the information you are getting from your left-hand opponent's play; you decide what is safe to throw by what he throws. Yet if his throws for the most part were identical with yours (and presumably you have been discarding odd low cards, so that you cannot continue making the same discards but must make new ones each time) you would find yourself completely in the dark as to what other cards were safe to throw to him. Remember that your early discard may be on a small pack, but by the time your right-hand opponent makes his next play there will be three more cards in the discard pile, and with each round of play his need for a safe discard becomes more desperate. As, of course, does yours.

The most important consideration always is the size of the discard pile and, secondarily, its value to your side. This matter of value is not so much what the pack contains as what you would have to sacrifice in order to retain some chance of getting it. It is almost always true that the side that takes the first pack of eight or more cards is the side that will win the hand. However, there are some hands where it is obvious that no matter what you do the opponents will have the best chance of getting the pack. Under these conditions you would be committing hari-kari if you engaged in a struggle which must go against you; you have to decide, as you watch the pack grow, whether your side must play all out for the pack or whether to risk a dangerous early discard which may give up the pack but which will retain your chances for going out as early as possible.

This is a matter of judgment which can only be acquired by your experience in play. The primary pitfalls to avoid are making melds which serve only to reduce your chances of getting the pack, and, at the opposite extreme, wrecking your hand in a hopeless battle to save a pack that, in the end, will prove beyond saving.

Timing and the initial meld: In two-handed play you have seen that there is practically no time when you should make the initial meld unless you are able to take the pack. In partnership play this is not true, especially where the minimum is at 120, but also when it is at lesser amounts. However, this does not mean that you should make the minimum meld for your side at great sacrifice to the number of cards you hold, except where you are forced to make the meld as the necessary play.

Nevertheless, it is generally advisable to make the initial meld for your side just as early as you are able to do so at small sacrifice. There are a few rare situations where you may hold back for a round or two because your hand is such that it affords a good chance to take the pack at the same time you make the minimum meld, but for the most part this advantage may be offset by the extra chance your partner will have if you unfreeze the pack for him by making your minimum meld early. The deciding factor should always be the effect that making the initial meld will have upon your side's present and future ability to gain the pack.

Thus, you may decide to postpone making a high initial meld for one or two rounds because the opponents will not suspect your ability to do so at such early stage; in this case if you made the meld it might warn them to be particularly careful of their discards, but withholding it may let you take the pack at the time you make the meld.

The ideal situation, however, comes when you can make the initial meld and still leave yourself with a wild card and a fair number of miscellaneous single cards; then by melding you *increase* your chances of taking the pack even if you *reduce* the number of cards you hold. The opponents' only countermoves are to place themselves on an equal footing by making what may be uneconomical melds themselves (which, however, will not affect your chances of gaining the pack), or they may have to discard a wild card which perhaps they can ill afford, thus freezing the pack for both sides. Remember, wild cards are especially valuable when a high figure is needed for the initial meld.

Still a third factor governs the decision to meld: how many safe discards you will be able to make from your shortened hand. If you still hold two or three safe cards, then why not increase your partner's chance of taking the pack by unfreezing it for him? But if making the minimum meld will put you in almost immediate jeopardy you will make the meld only if no other course seems to offer any hope.

The fourth factor is one that hardly needs mention: there is no point to taking the pack if there is no pack. Don't take a one or two-card pack to make the initial meld unless you can make it economically. Generally, don't take a one-card pack unless it gives you a chance to meld aces or it gives you a solid base for your first canasta. You will have a better chance of improving your hand by drawing from the stock.

Making the base: Of course the first important objective after making the initial meld is to complete a canasta. In this you have your partner's help; he will add cards to your melds, or you can add them to his. But if you make more than one meld, or if you have no meld which includes more than two or three natural cards, he cannot tell which of the melds he should try to build. You can use only three wild cards in forming the canasta; therefore you must have at least four natural cards. Whenever you can do so, you should indicate to your partner the best base for a canasta by putting down the fourth natural card of a meld.

In some cases it is good strategy to withhold cards of the same rank you have melded. This is especially true when you can hold up a pair of them (which may enable you to take a frozen pack) or when the matching card may have to be saved against the possibility you may have no other safe discard. However, as a rule don't postpone putting down the natural cards which will form the canasta base. Let your partner know where to add his wild cards if he decides your best strategy is to make a canasta and go out fast.

Partnership coöperation: It is impossible to win at Canasta unless both partners play the same game. If one player is obviously trying to keep the deal alive it is folly for his partner to suddenly decide to go out. On the other hand, if one partner has ruined his hand in order to make it possible to go out fast, it is usually suicide for the other partner to try to keep the deal going even though he has a good hand.

There are few conventional signals in Canasta, but one unmistakable one is when a player puts down all his cards but one. He wants out, and you had better help him if you are his partner, for his discards will surely enable the opponents to grab the pack. Another signal to the same effect is when a player deliberately adds a wild card or so to a meld, putting you close to but not completing a canasta. He is begging you to complete that canasta as soon as possible you must do so even at the expense of using wild cards you had hoped to meld in combination with cards in your own hand. Don't make your melds unless you can do so and still complete the canasta. But if you can complete the canasta, table as many additional melds as possible to give him additional chances to go out.

It is worthy of special warning however to caution you against reducing your hand if you cannot complete that canasta. Go as far as you can to complete it but hold as big a hand as you can; if both partners are playing with reduced hands they are at the mercy of the opponents and with bad luck the opponents may run out the entire pack without their ever being able to get that canasta completed.

One of the results of good partnership play is to get the opponents in a squeeze where they are unable to make any discards without giving your side the pack or so ruining their own hands that they give up all chance of going out. The ideal squeeze is one where your control of every rank virtually assures you the opponents cannot complete a canasta. If they cannot complete a canasta they cannot go out and you can prolong the deal to the bitter end. It is possible to score over 5,000 points on just one such deal.

In order to effect a squeeze, however, it is important for both the squeezers' hands to remain strong, so both partners must try to keep long hands. If one hand has been shortened his partner should make every effort to help him build it up again.

Another important factor in partnership play is the privilege of asking your partner, "May I go out?" Curiously enough, good players ask that question most often when they know the answer will be "No." They use this as a means of letting partner know that they are in a position to go out if he should decide, on his next turn, to meld what ever he has been holding up and let the deal end. Sometimes the question is asked merely to tell partner that you are in a position to complete your side's first canasta, without which he could not go out if he wanted to. This is a perfectly legitimate exchange of information since it also conveys the same news to your opponents, for whatever use they can make of it.

Of course you will also ask the question when you genuinely want your partner's advice. And in any case you must always be able to go out if he should answer affirmatively. Be careful about this; there's a drastic penalty for asking the question and then finding you can't deliver the goods if he says "Yes."

The point is that you rarely take the decision in your own hands and go out without asking. The exceptions are: when it is perfectly obvious that partner, too, is trying to go out as quickly as possible; when by going out you can catch the opponents by surprise and set them back, whereas if you asked and partner refused—which would mean that you would not be permitted to go out on that turn—the opponents might be able to scrape together some kind of meld before your next turn; and, if you are in a spot where you would have to make a disastrous discard if you did not go out.

There are two things about this business of asking which should also be emphasized. You don't have to ask at your next turn just because you have asked before. And you should not automatically assume because partner said "No" when you asked him last time that the situation hasn't changed by your next turn. You are entitled to keep right on asking, and you should do so.

Three other factors have considerable bearing upon your Canasta strategy and they are three things which give considerable opportunity for expertness: the state of the score, the number of cards still in each player's hand, and the number of cards remaining in the stock.

Playing to the score: The condition of the score should always be the factor to decide whether to play to go out quickly or to play on as long as possible. Sometimes, with a poor hand, you will try to go out fast purely as a defensive measure, but otherwise the score alone should control your decision. Thus, it seldom pays to play to set the opponents back. When you have that good a hand usually, if you keep on playing, you can roll up a big score of your own. However, when the opponents are close to 5,000 and you are considerably behind it may pay to go out, sacrificing the opportunity to make one or two extra canastas, if it does not appear likely that you yourself will be able to win the game on that particular deal.

In a more limited sense, the state of your own score, without regard to the opponents', may also decide this question. If you can hold your score to just below 1,500, or, more particularly, to just below 3,000, you will be able to start the next deal requiring a smaller initial meld. That is a consideration which may be worth several hundred points.

The condition of the score will have even more weighty influence on your play when you are close to 5,000 points. It is worth considerable risk to prolong the deal if by so doing you may be able to make the one extra canasta which will put your score over 5,000. Remember that once the next deal is begun it must be played to a conclusion, and during that deal your opponents may score several thousand points. When the score is such that the opponents cannot go over 5,000 but you can, keep a favorable deal going until you have achieved that 5,000 point goal.

Cards in other players' hands: The number of cards each player holds is very important to your strategy. It is hardly necessary to remind you that if your partner has a great many cards in his hand while both opponents are much reduced you should do everything possible to prolong the game; if you both have large hands it is doubly important to do so, even at the possible sacrifice of a few hundred points should the opponents be lucky enough to go out. The partnership with the greatest number of cards has the advantage always.

Specifically, there is the matter of position play. When your right hand opponent has just melded and thereby reduced his hand, it is a temptation for you to meld, even though it also reduces your hand, in order to put your side on equal terms. Don't yield to that temptation. Wait at least for one round to see if your partner is not able to make the meld. Here is why:

Suppose you reduce your hand. You will then be discarding from a short hand, always an increasingly difficult problem, into the long hand of your left-hand opponent. But if your partner is able to make the initial meld, he will be discarding from his shortened hand into the opponent who is already short and therefore less likely to be able to take his discards. Meanwhile you will have the benefit of the short-handed opponent discarding into your full hand.

Here is another pointer which many experienced Canasta players fail to consider. There is danger to the side which has the squeeze on its opponents if one of the partners has only a few cards while the other has a big hand. The partner with the short hand has a limited choice of discards; he may be forced to throw a card which will let the trapped opponents escape. Usually in such a situation the partner with the big hand can take the pack practically every time it is his turn, but if he does so his partner will never have a chance at anything bigger than a two-card pack and can never increase his hand. It is a fine point of expert play to pass up a small pack every now and again in the hope that the partner with few cards can take it.

Remember, however, this advice applies only to the situation where your side has so many melds on the table it is almost impossible for the opponents to discard without matching one of your melds. That is the factor that gives your short-handed partner his chance to take the pack. Naturally, you dare not a big pack get by you, but a two or three card pack will be four or five card pack by the time it reaches your partner.

Cards in the stock: The number of cards left in the stock is like the seconds on the timekeeper's watch in a football game. Once the cards have run out, time has run out. You are entitled to count the cards remaining in stock at any time, and you should do so particularly toward the end of a hand because you cannot make a meld if you do not get another turn. Only the other day I saw a player carefully count out that the four cards remaining in stock would surely give him another turn forgetting that one of them must be a red three because only three were on the table.

However, when you have the opponents in a squeeze don't let the dwindling stockpile rush you into making premature melds. It is toward the end of the hand that you may have the opponents really gasping: they may be forced to throw you another canasta with every discard. Frequently, in fact, when the stock has been exhausted you can continue the forcing process by discarding a card which will match the opponents' doubled melds. In that case, with no cards in stock, he is forced to take it and make still another discard to your partner. Sometimes it is possible to continue this forcing process with considerable profit for as long as two or three rounds of play.

Of course when there are a lot of cards in stock you prolong the game as much as possible if you have a good hand. But if you have a poor hand and you are in trouble, give the opponents something—anything—but try to keep your own hand in condition where you can go out and end the agony. You simply cannot afford to make safe plays that completely wreck your own chances if the number of cards left in the stock means that you are only postponing the inevitable unsafe ones. Only if the stock is very near the end should you consider breaking up your hand and "running out the clock." But be sure your "safe" discards will last, or you'll find your money won't.

HAND 1.

YOUR HAND (SOUTH)

East deals. Both sides need 50. You have just draw

QUESTION: Should you make an initial meld of
and 9-9-9?

ANSWER: No. As a rule, don't expend more th
cards to make an initial meld of 50, if you don't take t
at the same time. A hand depleted to less than seven c
little prospect of contributing to the subsequent earr
the partnership.

QUESTION: What should you discard?

ANSWER: In previous examples shown in the sec
two-hand play you have seen that it is often advisable
card from a trio, especially a trio of low cards. Here, h
you have two trios of high cards in what is a poor han

chances of getting the pack are small; on the other hand if the opponents take it after you have thrown a king or a nine you will have the additional discarding problem of being unable g- get rid of your remaining two cards of that rank. Your best play is to throw the four. However, with only one card in the pack, this is a case where it might be advisable to throw a loose high card—even the ace! With no wild card in your own hand your chance of being able to use your ace is remote; if you have to give, you might as well give immediately.

HAND 2.

YOUR HAND (SOUTH)

East deals. Both sides need 50. You have just drawn.

QUESTION: Should you make an initial meld of A-A-A?

ANSWER: On the first round, no; as soon as there are five or more cards in the pack, yes. This meld of only three cards is the most economical possible. The principal reason for not melding automatically, whenever you can, is that the cards if held in the hand may enable you to get the pack—not knowing you have the set, your right-hand neighbor may discard a card of the same rank. But this reason scarcely applies to aces. These are the only non-wild cards that count 20, so that they are almost never discarded "blind." You can hardly hope to catch an additional ace by concealing the set. The reason for waiting for the pack to build up a little is that your meld will make it easier for your partner to take the pack; even though you have no wild card, the chances are more than 2 to 1 in favor of his having one.

QUESTION: Whether or not you meld, what do you discard?

ANSWER: Preferably one of your 10-point cards—K, Q, J, or 10. You must let one of them go sooner or later. Do it now, before your left-hand opponent has a further chance to pair high cards in his hand. Your seven is less likely to give him an initial meld, but hold it for your next discard so if he can take your higher discard he won't get a pack with it.

HAND 3.

YOUR HAND (SOUTH)

East deals. Both sides need 50. You have just made your first draw.

QUESTION: Should you make an initial meld of 2-Q-Q-Q?

ANSWER: Not immediately; as in Hand 2, it is better to wait a round or two. Perhaps you will draw another ace and be able to meld 2-A-A. There is even a remote chance that your neighbor will discard a queen. Still, a four-card meld is as economical as you can usually expect; plan to put it down as soon as the pack has grown a bit.

QUESTION: Should you discard a queen, since you could still make your initial meld whenever necessary?

ANSWER: No, since you are going down in a round or two, save your most economical meld.

HAND 4.

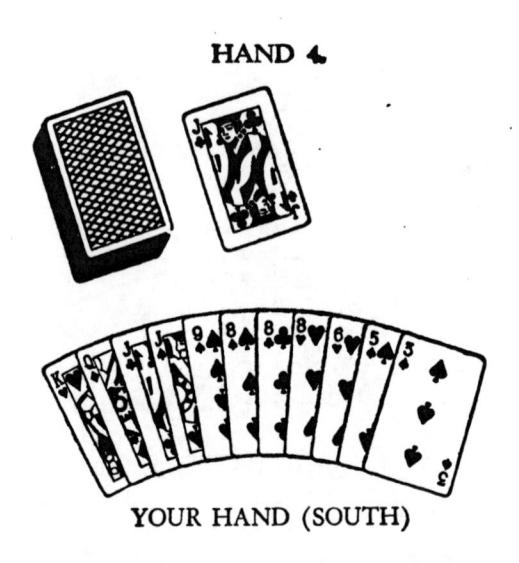

YOUR HAND (SOUTH)

East deals. Both sides need 50. It is your first play.

QUESTION: Should you take the up-card to meld J-J-J and 8-8-8 for an initial meld?

ANSWER: No. The argument stated in Hand 1 applies. Though it seems a pity to miss the chance to fill the jacks, melding six cards to do so is a poor investment. If there were two or three cards under the jack, you would take it.

Canasta for Four 69

HAND 5.

YOUR HAND (SOUTH)

East deals. Both sides need 50. It is your first play.

QUESTION: Should you take the up-card to meld A-A-A?

ANSWER: Yes. Don't pass up the opportunity to fill the aces and make the most economical initial meld.

QUESTION: Having melded, what should you discard?

ANSWER: The 4 or 7—take your choice. Don't waste your black trey this time. A standard Canasta maxim is, "Having made your initial meld, discard a black three to save the pack for your partner"—but this applies to situations in which there is some sort of pack to save. Another maxim is, "The right time to discard a black three is any time you have one"—but this applies to times when you are saving your live cards in hopes of getting the pack. This time there's no pack to get.

HAND 6.

YOUR HAND (SOUTH)

East deals. You need 50. It is your first play.

QUESTION: Should you take the up-card and meld 2-J-J-J-J?

ANSWER: Yes. Don't pass up the base for a canasta (four natural matching cards), even when it takes five cards out of your hand. If it took six cards, the play would be optional; seven cards, it would not be worthwhile. It is particularly important to you that the pack be unfrozen early because you still have a wild card and you have several unmatched cards. In other words, by making the initial meld you have sacrificed four cards from your hand, but you have at the same time increased your chance of regaining these cards by being able to take the pack.

HAND 7.

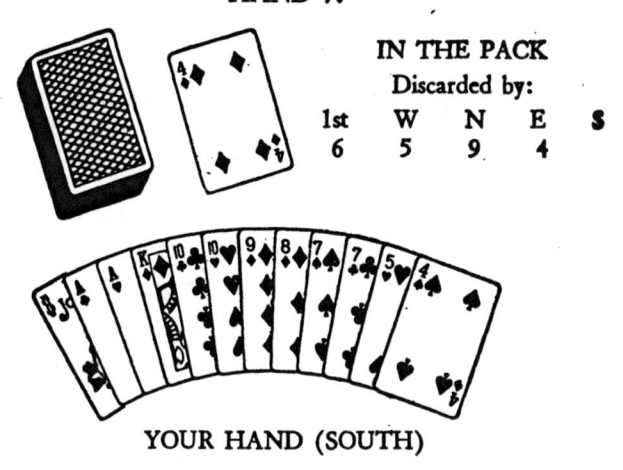

IN THE PACK
Discarded by:

	1st	W	N	E	S
	6	5	9	4	

YOUR HAND (SOUTH)

You dealt. Both sides need 90. You have just drawn a 9.

QUESTION: Should you make an initial meld of Joker-A-A?

ANSWER: Yes. This is the ideally-economical meld for 90. Put it down at once, to unfreeze the pack for your partner (who probably has a wild card) and so saddle a defensive burden on the opponents.

QUESTION: What do you discard now?

ANSWER: Either the 4 or the 5. However, you should lean toward the 4 on the first round, reserving the 5 for the next round, on the theory that since West (your left-hand opponent) discarded a five on his first play it will be a safe card when the pack is a little larger on the next round. Note also that by following your right-hand opponent's discard of a four you do not give him information regarding cards he can safely throw to you.

HAND 8.

IN THE PACK
Discarded by:

1st	S	W	N	E
Q	4	4	7	6
	10	3	5	10
	4	3	5	8

YOUR HAND (SOUTH)

East dealt. Both sides need 90. You have just drawn a 9.

QUESTION: Should you make an initial meld of K-K-K, J-J-J, and 9-9-9?

ANSWER: Perish the thought! To do so would cripple your hand. Don't meld nine cards for 90 (without taking the pack) except as the last resort of desperation. Play along to get wild cards or a helpful discard from your neighbor.

QUESTION: What should you discard?

ANSWER: Your 5 seems best; your partner threw two of them. At this point, with the pack so large, every discard should be chosen for safety, but as long as possible you should hold your three sets. Any of them may start you toward a canasta, if partner can go down.

HAND 9.

YOUR HAND (SOUTH)

East deals. Both sides need 90. You have just drawn from the stock for your first play.

QUESTION: Should you make an initial meld of 2-A-A and 8-8-8?

ANSWER: Not immediately. Compare Hand 3. Though you must usually expect to spend as many as six cards to make 90, don't be in a hurry about it. Wait a few rounds to see what develops. Maybe you will catch another 8. But be ready to go down as soon as your partner seems to have discarding difficulties.

QUESTION: What do you discard?

ANSWER: The 7 or 6—as in Hand 5, save the black trey to discard when you make your initial meld, which you are sure to do in two more rounds.

HAND 10.

IN THE PACK
Discarded by:
1st W N E S
6   4 5 4

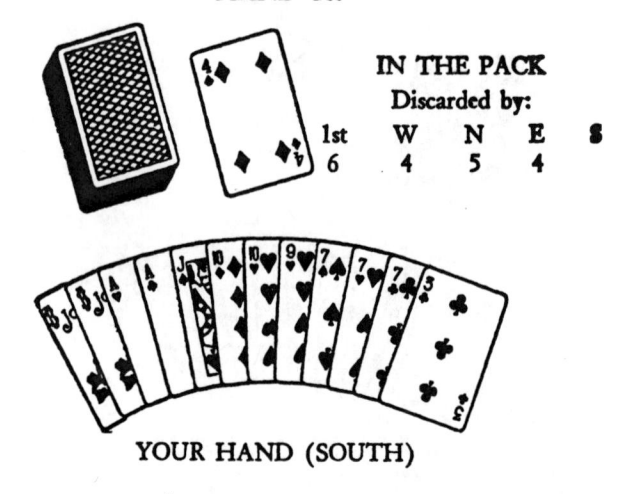

YOUR HAND (SOUTH)

You dealt. Both sides need 120. You have just drawn a joker.

QUESTION: Should you make an initial meld?

ANSWER: No; wait one or two more rounds. To make 120 with only four cards is almost miraculous. It is precisely for this reason that you can afford to wait. The tactical advantage to your side in melding first is greater at 120 than at 90 or 50. You exploit this advantage best when the pack is larger.

Discard a 7. Save the black trey; it will be more valuable later.

QUESTION: When you do meld, should it be your jokers and aces, your jokers and tens, or Joker-A-A and Joker-10-10?

ANSWER: Only the jokers and aces. You would meld the tens if you did not have the aces, but aces are always preferred when there is a choice. The opponents, needing 120, must save aces anyway—they will not throw you one. They may throw a ten, giving you the pack. That's why you hold the tens.

HAND 11.

YOUR HAND (SOUTH)

East deals. Both sides need 120. It is your first play, and you have just drawn a 7.

QUESTION: Should you make an initial meld of Joker-Q-Q, 10-10-10-2?

ANSWER: No. It is true that the tactical advantage of melding first at 120 is worth a big investment—even seven cards. But here there is potential advantage in holding back a while.

In this hand the big advantage of not melding at once is that you improve your chance of being thrown a 5. Once you meld, your right-hand opponent will be very careful of his discards and will try to make them especially safe; if you have made no meld, because the minimum is at 120 he will throw low cards freely. After your right-hand neighbor rids his hand of low cards, he may eventually be forced to discard a high card— which may be a queen or ten. Discard your 4 or 6; the 7 may be a somewhat safer discard later, when the pack has grown.

HAND 12.

YOUR HAND (SOUTH)

East deals. Both sides need 120. It is your first play.

QUESTION: Should you take the up-card and make an initial meld of 2-A-A-A and 8-8-8-8?

ANSWER: Yes. It is not a play without its disadvantages—to leave yourself only three cards is dangerous. Yet can you afford to pass up the chance to get the ace? If you let it go, your chance of making a more economical meld appears to depend on drawing a joker. Fortunes have been lost on this vain hope! While you wreck your own hand by melding, your partner's remains intact, and he will have a far better chance than either opponent to get the pack, perhaps again and again. It is better to "take the cash and let the credit go"—grab the ace, meld, and hope your pair of fives will put you back in the game. Discard your king; save your 4 until next time, when the opponent may hold a pair of kings he does not have now.

HAND 13.

YOUR HAND (SOUTH)

East deals. Both sides need 120. It is your first play.

QUESTION: Should you take the up-card and meld your aces, tens, fours, and deuce?

ANSWER: You might think that the answer would depend on the score. For example, if the score were, say 4,500 for them to 3,200 for you, and if they have a couple of red threes, it is persuasive to play for a quick out. You figure on going down at once, leaving yourself with only one card, and thereby asking partner to build one of your melds to a canasta as fast as possible, meld what he can, and wait for you to draw a player. You'd then begin the next deal approximately on even terms with the opponents. And if it worked out that way all would be well.

But actually this play is too dangerous. First of all, your partner has to be able to build a quick canasta. He may not be able to do that for some time, but in trying to do so he may also wreck his hand. Then you are at the mercy of the opponents and they will win the game with a huge score. Meanwhile, since they already have 300 points (in red threes) toward the 500 they need, you will let one of them make an initial meld, however expensively to his hand, without much risk.

You have too good a hand to sacrifice it this early. You already have 105 points and an ace, a wild card, or a ten will let you make the minimum meld at any time. Meanwhile by refusing the ten at this point you increase the chances that your opponent will throw one to you. Don't give away the situation by thinking too long. Draw from stock and let your draw decide what you will discard. If possible, however, hang on to your fours until you no longer need them to make up a possible 120 minimum.

HAND 14.

YOUR HAND (SOUTH)

East deals. Both sides need 50. You draw a Queen.

QUESTION: What should you discard?

ANSWER: The 3. The 6 and 5 are apparently useless, but the 3 is even more useless, as concerns meld-making and pack-getting. The only question is: should the 3 be saved up for possible emergency? The answer is: no. It was different (Hands 5 and 9) when you had your minimum and could make your initial meld when you chose. This time you are out to make combinations, and you'll never make one with a three-spot.

HAND 15.

	IN THE PACK Discarded by:			
1st	S	W	N	E
	A	4	10| 7	J
	7	6	5	4
	3	8	Q	3

YOUR HAND (SOUTH)

Both sides need 50. East (your right-hand opponent) has just made the initial meld for his side, putting down 2-9-9-9. You have drawn from the stock.

QUESTION: Do you meld 2-K-K (or 2-10-10) and 6-6-6?

ANSWER: No. Wait one round to see if your partner can make the initial meld for your side. If he can, you will not be in the position of having to discard each time from a "short" hand (five cards) into West's full hand of eleven cards, while East, with seven cards to your five, would have a greater choice of discards than you. For you to meld now would in no way reduce your problem of what to discard this time.

But it is urgent, since your opponents have gone down, for your side to equalize matters by making your initial meld. So if at his next turn your partner can't meld, you might meld at your next turn even though six of your cards be required.

Canasta for Four

QUESTION: What do you discard?

ANSWER: One of your 6s seems safest, but they are essential to your initial meld if you must make it on the next round, and your draw may not be favorable. East's meld put you at a temporary disadvantage; you must bear it and risk having the pack taken; and so probably will your partner in his turn. Take a chance on discarding a 10—West threw one, and while it is possible that he split a trio or a pair, or that he has since drawn a 10, none of these is likely.

If you get away with it, you may then decide to postpone melding on your next turn because you still have a safe discard—your remaining 10.

HAND 16.

IN THE PACK
Discarded by:

1st	N	E	S	W
A	4	10	7	J
	10	6	5	4
	3	8	K	3
	7	5		

YOUR HAND (SOUTH)

Both sides need 50. West (your left-hand opponent) made the initial meld for his side at his last turn, putting down 2-9-9-9. You have drawn from the stock.

QUESTION: Do you make the initial meld for your side, with the deuce and two of your high cards, plus 4-4-4?

ANSWER: Yes. It is important to put your side on even terms with the opponents, as regards getting the pack, as soon as you can. Compare this with Hand 15; it is the same type of hand, the same problem, but the position is different. This time, while you must expend six cards to meld, you are only two cards worse off than West, while your partner retains his full hand.

QUESTION: Do you meld the queens or the 9s?

ANSWER: In this case the Qs. Superficially, it would seem to be advantageous to have a convenient parking place for your 9s—the rank the opponents have already melded. However, consider the three possibilities: (1) If the deck is frozen, holding queens in your hand is scarcely more likely to get you the pack than the 9s would be AND you will be able to discard your nines in relative safety. (2) If the opponents get the pack it will be disastrous anyway, but far more so if you have made a meld which you are unlikely to be able to build into a canasta. The queens at least offer far more hope in that direction. (3) If your side gets the pack it doesn't much matter.

QUESTION: Having melded 2-Q-Q and 4-4-4, what do you discard?

ANSWER: Your jack, remembering that West discarded one early. If he was advertising, holding a pair of jacks still in his hand, then he has put one over on you; but this is sufficiently unlikely to allow you to take a chance. Although the pack is no longer frozen, you have no wild card and until you draw one you want to hold your pairs as your only chance of taking it.

Canasta for Four 83
HAND 17.

	IN THE PACK			
	Discarded by:			
1st	W	N	E	S
	5	5	7	8

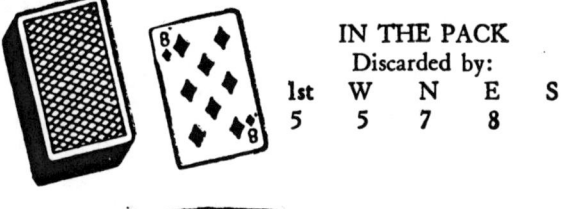

YOUR HAND (SOUTH)

You need 90; West (your left-hand opponent) at his last turn melded Joker-A-A.

QUESTION: Do you make the initial meld for your side?

ANSWER: No. It would take at least seven cards, while West has not seriously depleted his hand and would be in a good position to take the discards you would have to make from your short hand. The pack is still small and it is no insurmountable tragedy if an opponent gets it. You would be little better off if you melded and freed the pack for your side: For one thing, you would need both your wild cards to make your meld; another consideration is that your cards are paired and if you can get the pack at all, you can probably get it anyway.

QUESTION: What do you discard?

ANSWER: The 5. It looks fairly safe, since West previously discarded one. Your black trey may be more valuable if the pack builds up in the next two rounds or so.

HAND 18.

IN THE PACK
Discarded by:

1st	W	N	E	S
A	K	Q	6	4
	9	9	4	7
	4	6	J	9
	7	4	9	3
	3	7	3	

YOUR HAND (SOUTH)

With both sides needing 90, East has just gone down with a joker and four kings, and has discarded the black three. You have drawn from the stock.

QUESTION: What do you discard?

ANSWER: Discard a deuce, freezing the pack.

Deliberately freezing the pack is a ticklish matter. At best it costs a wild card, and a wild card expended may eventually make the difference of a canasta—300 points. Your advantage from a frozen pack may be offset, or even outweighed, by the damage it does your partner if he soon proves to have an economical initial meld and a wild card in his remaining cards. But the compensating advantage is constant: It restores equality, when the opponents have gone down and you have not, so that they cannot get the pack more easily than you can.

In this case, you cannot make a 90-point meld with your

hand as it is, and it is unlikely that any card you draw, except a joker, would persuade you to; for in any other case you would have to use at least seven cards. If you draw a joker, you can reach the minimum in spite of having thrown a deuce.

But the most important consideration is this: If you do not throw the deuce, what safe discard have you? With a safe discard you would gladly wait for at least one round and hope your partner might meld, or that at least he too could discard safely. But of your unpaired cards, neither a 5 nor a 10 has shown in the discards, and you could not even consider yourself safe if you broke one of your pairs. When there are approximately twenty cards in the pack, giving it to the opponents is fatal.

If the deuce were your only wild card, you probably would save it and take a chance on a dangerous discard. If you had three wild cards, instead of two, you probably would be willing to sacrifice one without question. Therefore the problem usually arises when you have two wild cards, as in this case.

Having postponed your agony over the immediate discard, by your next turn you may have some clue to what is safe. If no better clue materializes, probably your best bet is to split your 6s since two of these have already turned up in the discards.

HAND 19.

	IN THE PACK			
	Discarded by:			
1st	W	N	E	8
	A	K	Q	6	4
	9	9	4	7
	4	6	J	9
	7	4	9	3
	3	2	5	

YOUR HAND (SOUTH)

With both sides needing 90, West (your left-hand opponent) went down in his last turn with a joker and four kings. North (your partner) and East drew and discarded, North discarding a deuce to freeze the pack, East discarding a 5. You have already drawn from the stock.

QUESTION: What do you discard?

ANSWER: The ace! It's a safe discard; unless West is unusually tricky he wouldn't have melded the four kings with his joker, using five cards, if he could have melded the joker and two aces instead, using only three. When the pack is so large, you try to make every discard safe and hope for the best. You look ahead if you can, but the urgency of the present discard supersedes all other considerations.

HAND 20.

YOUR HAND (SOUTH)

You need 90, the opponents 120. There are about a dozen cards in the pack. You have just drawn your joker.

QUESTION: Do you make your initial meld with Joker-8-8-8-8?

ANSWER: Yes, indeed. A joker and 10-point cards are about as economical a meld as you can hope for when you need 90. Aces are better, but you haven't even one ace. It might take you the rest of the game to get two of them.

QUESTION: Why not Joker-2-8-8, using fewer cards and saving a pair of eights as a deceptive measure?

ANSWER: Several reasons why not. If you meld the joker and 8s, the pack is unfrozen for you—a factor that becomes meaningless if you haven't a wild card. So you want to save a wild card in your hand. Then, while there is an occasional advantage to hiding in your hand a pair of the same rank you have melded, it is unlikely to operate in this case. The pack is not frozen; the opponents, needing 120 for their own initial meld, probably cannot spare a high-counting wild card to freeze it; and so long as the pack is not frozen for you, there is no chance that East will throw you an 8 anyway, for that would give you the pack. Finally, it clarifies matters for your partner when you show him the base for a canasta, four natural matching cards.

QUESTION: After melding the joker and 8s, what do you discard?

ANSWER: A king or a 9, whichever seems safer. This is a time (when the pack is unfrozen and you have a wild card) to split your pairs and keep as many different ranks of card in your hand as possible. For taking the pack, a pair will be of no more value than a single card plus your wild card.

HAND 21.

YOUR HAND (SOUTH)

With both sides needing 120, East (your right-hand opponent) has just made his initiail meld with Joker-9-9 and A-A-A. There are nine cards in the pack. You have just drawn from the stock.

QUESTION: Should you discard a deuce and freeze the pack?

ANSWER: No. Although we said in Hand 18 (where the initial requirement was only 90) that when you hold three deuces you can spare one, this is not the case when you need 120, and the right-hand opponent has already gone down, using one or more wild cards. With four or more of the wild cards accounted for, your partner is going to have difficulty making 120; you may be the only one who will ever be able to do so for your side. In this case, although you would like to freeze the pack you dare not do so because you must keep every possible chance to make the minimum meld and you will need all your wild cards. If you draw a king, jack, ten, or eight you will be able to make the minimum meld (however expensively). And, with your right-hand opponent reduced to five cards there is a good chance of his having to throw you a ten or an eight enabling you to take the pack while you meld your minimum.

If you had only one, or possibly, two deuces with this type of hand (where you would not be close to your required 120 in any case) it might be advisable for you to freeze the pack, to give your partner greater freedom in discarding and to reduce the chances of either opponent's being able to take the deck.

Unless there is some indication from the discards that the king or jack is safe, throw the seven and play along. Even if the opponents take the pack at this stage, it is not necessarily fatal.

HAND 22.

YOUR HAND (SOUTH)

Both sides have melded:
Your melds, A-A-A-2, K-K-K-Joker, 7-7-7-7-7, 5-5-5-5-2.
Their melds, A-A-Joker, Q-Q-Q-Q, 9-9-9-2.

West, like you, is down to four cards (before drawing); East has nine cards; your partner, who got the pack, has thirteen. There are about a dozen cards in the pack, which is not frozen.

QUESTION: Do you meld 10-10-2?

ANSWER: Of course not. The discard of either other card, which would then be forced, gives West the pack.

QUESTION: Do you add your deuce to the 5s or 7s?

ANSWER: No. That would be a play to go out. You have the advantage (more melds, more cards) and should play to prolong the game and get the pack again.

QUESTION: What do you discard?

ANSWER: The deuce. It is a safe discard, and gives you two more probably safe discards, the queen and 9, once the pack is frozen. Your partner, with the most cards and with a short hand discarding to him, still has the best chance to get the pack, and—with fourteen cards to select from each time—the least danger of throwing it to the opponents. Since you retain a pair (10s) you even have a remote chance of getting it yourself!

HAND 23.

```
          IN THE PACK
          Discarded by:
       1st  S   W   N   E
       2, A 5   6   5   4
            7   5   4   7
            4   10  3   3
```

YOUR HAND (SOUTH)

You needed 90, the opponents 120. North (your partner) on his last turn went down with Joker-2-Q-Q; but the pack is still frozen by the deuce originally turned. You have just drawn.

QUESTION: Do you add your queens to partner's meld?

ANSWER: No, because the pack is frozen. Pairs are precious, and a queen will look like a safe discard to East, since your partner melded two of them.

QUESTION: Do you meld your sixes?

ANSWER: No, even though they are a base for a canasta. The fact that there are five 6s out (your quartet, and one in the pack) may greatly reduce the likelihood that one will be thrown to you; but by the same token a 6 becomes a safe discard for you.

Canasta for Four 93

QUESTION: So what do you discard?

ANSWER: A 6. You have a double advantage in this deal: You got the jump by melding first, and the opponents need 120. Don't think about that canasta of 6s; you want several canastas. And your nicely-paired hand is wonderful when the pack is frozen.

HAND 24.

YOUR HAND (SOUTH)

The opponents need 50; your partner just made your initial meld, taking a four-card pack and putting down 2-K-K and 10-10-10. In addition to the 4 just discarded by East, the pack contains only one card, your partner's discard of a 6.

QUESTION: Do you take the 4 to meld with your pair of 4s?

ANSWER: No; even though it gives you a meld at the

94   *How to Play Canasta*

expense of only one card it is not worth missing a draw to take a one or two card deck. There's always a chance you might draw a joker.

QUESTION: You draw, say a nine. Do you meld your 7s and (with your wild card) your jacks?

ANSWER: No, neither of them. There is no hurry about the 7s. The wild card is essential to your hand, with the pack unfrozen.

QUESTION: Do you add your 10 to partner's meld?

ANSWER: Yes. The base for a canasta should be revealed to partner as soon as possible (there being exceptions, of course, as in Hand 23).

HAND 25.

YOUR HAND (SOUTH)

Both sides began the deal with about 3,500, needing 120. On his first turn North (your partner) put down A-A-A, K-K-K,

8-8-8-8, reducing himself to one card. Each side has one red three. In the pack are 5, 4, 9, 6, 6 (including the top discard).

QUESTION: Do you take the pack with your 6 and a wild card?

ANSWER: No. It would give you a three-card meld at the expense of a wild card. Your partner's unusual play, in stripping his hand to one card, establishes the strategy for your side: You must go out at once, to set the opponents back while advancing your own score, even though slightly. Your partner's remaining card might be a wild card (but he could not play it before because, without a canasta, he could not legally go out). You must add your king to his meld, and add both your wild cards to either the kings or the 8s. Then discard the black three.

HAND 26.

YOUR HAND (SOUTH)

With both sides needing 90, East has taken a big pack. The opponents' melds are A-A-A-A-2, 8-8-8-Joker, 4-4-4-4, 6-6-6-

96   *How to Play Canasta*

6-6-6-6 (natural canasta). At his last turn your partner melded 7-7-7-7-7 and 9-9-Joker. West still has nine cards, while East has more than he started with.

QUESTION: Do you meld anything?

ANSWER: Not your kings or 5s; not your pair with your deuces; but you do add a deuce to your partner's meld of 7s. The opponents are too far ahead of you, in this deal, for you to have any hope of catching them. You must go out as soon as possible. Your play on the 7s tells partner to add a wild card to that meld if he has one; it will complete a canasta and make it legally possible for you to go out upon drawing any matching card.

Of course you are going to discard the queen. Then, on your next round even if partner is unable to complete the canasta, you may draw a wild card or a ten which would release the wild card you already have and enable you to complete the canasta yourself and go out. If your situation does not improve within a couple of rounds, it might be advisable for you to use your deuce to complete the canasta and hope your partner can go out. If by then he is down to one or two cards, make your other melds at the same time in order to give him additional chances to meld out.

HAND 27.

YOUR HAND (SOUTH)

Both sides need 50. It is your second play; a king was turned, and the discards are 7, 10, 5, 3 and 4 (the present top card).

QUESTION: Should you take the pack and meld 2-9-9 (or 2-8-8) and 4-4-4?

ANSWER: Yes. You will have made the initial meld and still have ten cards in your hand. The fact that you have used your only wild card, is unfortunate; because the advantage to your own hand of having the pack unfrozen thereby vanishes. But you have a partner, and his chance of getting the next pack is increased; and by the time the pack grows again to something worth taking, you may have drawn a wild card.

The fact that not one of the cards you get from the pack will match a card in your hand is inconsequential. In Canasta there is usually an advantage to having as many cards as possible, even if they are temporarily unmatched; your future draws will take care of that.

HAND 28.

YOUR HAND (SOUTH)

The opponents need 120 and have not melded. You need 90 and have melded A-A-A-A-A-Joker, 5-5-5, and 9-9-9-9-2. Your partner has seven cards, while each opponent of course has eleven.

You take the pack with your pair of 8s. There are twenty-nine cards in it, and you find yourself with this assortment, including the cards you already had:

    2 2 Joker (there was a deuce in the pack)
    3 3 3 (black, of course)
    4 4 4 4
    5 5 5
    6 6 6 6
    7 7 7 7 7

9
10 10 10 10 10
J J
Q Q Q Q Q
K K

QUESTION: What do you meld?

ANSWER: Only what you can meld and still keep a pair in your hand. Put down three 7s, three 10s, three queens. Add a 5 to your previous meld; your partner, having seen you take the pack, knows you still have two of them and can complete a natural canasta if he has one 5 to add. Add your 9 to the five you already have, so that your partner can complete that canasta if he is able to.

Holding up all these cards is not without its dangers. The opponents are obviously on the run; neither has been able to amass 120 points. But either may be very close to it and his partner may be able to complete a canasta and go out before you get another turn. Then your real loss will not be the cards left in your hand—a few hundred inconsequential points—but the score you could have made by completing some canastas. You and your partner between you could undoubtedly make three or four canastas at once.

That is the gamble you take when you hold up a big hand. Every now and then you will lose by it. But in the long run you will gain far more. There are ten or twelve good cards that the opponents must still throw you sooner or later, and they will almost surely mean three or four more canastas for you. If you stripped your hand of pairs now, an opponent could freeze the pack and then safely make discards that match your melds. Perhaps they would find enough such discards to prevent your ever getting the pack again.

The degree of danger depends on how many canastas are available to the opponents. In this case, 8s, jacks and kings are open. It is also conceivable for an opponent to make a canasta of 4s or 6s, since you know the whereabouts of only four cards in each of those ranks, but it is, after all, unlikely that the opponents hold all four missing cards in either.

QUESTION: Should you add your joker to the aces and make at least one canasta?

ANSWER: Yes. You would like to wait and see whether you cannot complete the canasta of aces with a natural card. But you are being greedy enough. It is usually advisable to complete the first canasta for your side if you can do so without great sacrifice and you will still have two wild cards left in your hand. Of course you use the joker, rather than one of the deuces, because at this stage the 50-point count is better melded than still in your hand.

QUESTION: What do you discard?

ANSWER: A black three. Save all your live cards. You are unlikely to want to go out for three rounds. Certainly you do not want to discard a deuce; it is to your advantage, for the time being, to keep the pack unfrozen. Your opponents may throw you cards that match your melds, as the least of the evils available to them, and when such a card puts you closer to a canasta you or your partner will take it.

Canasta for Four

HAND 29.

YOUR HAND (NORTH)

You are the partner of the player who, in his last turn, took the big pack described in Hand 28. Your melds are A-A-A-A-A-Joker-Joker, Q-Q-Q, 10-10-10, 9-9-9-9-9-2, 8-8-8, 7-7-7 and 5-5-5-5. It is your turn and you draw a jack.

QUESTION: What do you do?

ANSWER: Ask your partner, "May I go out?" Obviously his answer will be "No," because he is holding up a mittful of cards and can complete some canastas if he gets one more turn. By your question you will tell him that you could go out if you wished (as you could, by completing a canasta of 9s, adding your 8s to the meld, melding 2-K-K and discarding the jack). On his next turn he may wish to complete a few canastas, meld what else he can, and let you end the play.

QUESTION: Is it ethical to ask when you know the answer will be No?

ANSWER: Yes, because your knowledge that partner will

answer No comes from the logic of the situation; the opponents know and understand this as well as you do. If you had a secret understanding with your partner that he should say No, that would be unethical.

QUESTION: After receiving partner's negative answer, what will you do?

ANSWER: Add your eights to the meld on the table, of course. Then complete the canasta of nines. But don't play both your nines. This second one is unnecessary and is far more valuable to give you an absolutely safe discard. Hold the deuce and two kings and the jack. It is true you are no longer in an "out" position, but it is not necessary for you to keep that position indefinitely; you must only be able to go out at the time you ask.

Of course it is desirable to keep in an out position once you have asked the question, so that if your partner then decides to put down a lot of melds you will be able to end the game. However, in this case with all the melds he can put down it is odds-on that you will be able to draw a matching card and go out by melding your kings and deuce and discarding your jack. Meanwhile, since no jacks have shown, that would be an extremely dangerous discard.

HAND 30.

YOUR HAND (SOUTH)

You need 120; your opponents need 90, but East (your right-hand opponent) has just taken a seven-card discard pile and has melded 2-A-A and 8-8-8. You have just drawn.

QUESTION: What do you discard?

ANSWER: Your ace. Don't dream of parting with a 6 or a 9, or of sacrificing a wild card to freeze the pack. You are in trouble on this hand. You need 120 and cannot hope to reach it without using almost your entire hand anyway; your partner may be no better off (and very likely is worse off, because after all you do have two deuces). The one bright spot is that you have a well-matched hand. Keep it that way and play to go out concealed. That means melding a canasta, and your 6s and 9s are the indispensable base. One more 6 or 9, or one more wild card and you are out. If in the meantime your opponents score enough to pull up even with you, at least they, like you, will need 120 on the next deal.

Of course, throwing an ace will add to the opposing meld and may eventually mean a canasta to them. What of it? For the next few rounds you will have to give them whatever cards you draw, anyway, unless those cards match the ones you have. If the opponents take one small pack after another, it will be no worse than having them take a big pack later. And if by chance your partner has a good hand, and can go down with your minimum, you can judge whether to shift your policy—and have a pretty good hand for the purpose, too.

You discard the ace rather than the eight despite the 10 point difference in value of these cards; the opponents' meld of aces already includes a wild card, their eights do not. Thus you prefer to let them make a mixed rather than a natural canasta. And, of at least equal if not greater importance, when you give them an ace you still have not given them the natural base they need for the canasta, but giving them an 8 would do so.

LAWS OF CANASTA

The following laws are the same in substance, though not necessarily in arrangement and wording, as the Canasta laws adopted by the Association of American Playing Card Manufacturers and by The Regency Club of New York.

Players

1. Canasta may be played by two, three, four, five, or six players. It is best for two or four.

2. (a) With two or three players, each plays for himself. With four or more players, there are two partnerships.

(b) With four, partners sit opposite each other at the table. With five, two partners are opposed by three, but only two of the three play at a time, rotating so that a different one of the three is idle each deal.

(c) With six players, three on each side, partners sit alternately around the table. With six players in three partnerships of two each, Three-pack Canasta is recommended—see page 00.

Cards

3. The game is played with two regular decks of 52 cards, plus four jokers, all 108 cards being shuffled together. (See also Three-pack Canasta, page 00.)

4. The jokers and deuces (twospots) are wild. A wild card may be designated to be of any rank, at the pleasure of the owner.

Preliminaries

5. (a) Partnerships may be determined by drawing cards from the deck, spread face down on the table. The two or three highest cards drawn show the partners playing against the other two or three. Highest card has choice of seats.

(b) For purposes of the draw only, the suits rank: Spades (high), Hearts, Diamonds, Clubs; and the cards of each suit rank: Ace (high), king, queen, jack, etc. to deuce (low). Jokers are void, in drawing. If two players draw cards of the same rank, they draw again to determine which of them is higher.

6. The player drawing the highest card plays first; therefore, the player at his right deals first. Thereafter the right to deal rotates to the left, clockwise.

7. The player at the right of the dealer cuts the deck, after any player who wishes to shuffle has done so. The dealer has the right to shuffle last. In cutting, each packet must comprise at least four cards.

8. The dealer gives eleven cards to each player one at a time clockwise, face down, beginning with the opponent at his left and ending with himself. (When there are three players, each receives thirteen cards; with two players, each receives fifteen.)

9. The undealt remainder of the deck is placed face down in the center of the table to form the stock. The top card of the stock is turned face up beside it; this is the up-card. All subsequent discards are laid face up in one pile, on the up-card, if the first player does not take it. Only the top discard may be seen.

10. If the up-card is a red trey or a wild card it must immediately be covered by another card from the top of the stock, and the discard pile is then frozen (see rule 31). Additional cards must be turned when necessary until the up-card is not a red trey or wild card.

Red Treys

11. The red treys (threespots) are bonus cards, counting for or against the side to which they fall, but never forming a part of the eleven-card hand. At his first turn to play, each player must withdraw from his hand each red trey dealt to him, put it face up on the table, then draw a card from the top of the stock to restore his hand to eleven cards. After this, he may draw and play as provided in rule 15.

12. On drawing a red trey from the stock, a player must immediately face the trey on the table and draw a replacement

from the stock to keep in his hand. A red trey taken in the discard pile is similarly faced, but is not replaced from the stock.

13. Each red trey has the point value of 100, except that if all four red treys are owned by one side each counts 200, or 800 points in all. After the play is finished, a side that has made any meld scores all its red treys as plus bonuses; a side that has made no meld has the value of its treys deducted from its score.

Order of Play

14. The opponent at the left of the dealer plays first; thereafter the turn passes to the left, clockwise. Each turn comprises: a draw, a meld (optional), and a discard.

15. The player in turn is always entitled to draw the top card of the stock; subject to restrictions given in the following sections, he may instead take the top card of the discard pile, if he can use it in a meld. Having so taken the last discard, he must take the entire pile and add it to his hand or his melds.

16. A discard must always be made from the hand, never from a meld. The act of discarding ends a player's turn, even though he should have failed to draw a card. (But see rule 53.)

17. The player whose turn it is, before he discards, may—

(a) count the number of cards in the stock (but he may not count the discard pile or see any card in it except the top card).

(b) ask any other player(s) how many cards that player has; and he is entitled to a correct answer to this question.

(c) announce that he has only one card left. (It is customary to make this announcement.)

Melds

18. (a) The principal object of play is to form melds, combinations of three or more cards of the same rank, with or without the help of wild cards. (Sequences are not valid melds in Canasta.)

(b) A meld is valid if it contains at least two natural (not wild) cards of the same rank, and not more than three wild cards. But black treys may not be melded unless the player goes out in the same turn. Jokers and deuces may never be melded separately from natural cards.

19. To count plus, a meld must be laid face up on the table, in some proper turn of the owner. Cards left in the hand when play ends, even though they might form melds, count minus. All the melds of both partners are placed before one of them.

20. A player may add one or more cards of the same rank or wild cards to a meld previously faced by himself or his partner. Wild cards in any number may be added to a completed canasta, but no other meld may contain more than three wild cards.

21. A player may make as many melds as he wishes in his turn, including the addition of cards to melds previously made by his side. A player may not add a card to a meld of the other side.

Canastas

22. A meld comprising seven or more cards is a canasta. A canasta may be built up by an initial meld of three or more cards and addition of other cards later. (The importance of a canasta is two-fold; it carries a special bonus, and a side must have at least one canasta before it can go out. In two-hand play, a player must have two canastas before he can go out.)

23. (a) Seven natural cards form a natural canasta, valued at 500. A canasta formed with help of one to three wild cards is mixed and is valued at 300.

(b) Additional cards added to a canasta do not increase the bonus, but merely add the point values of the cards. A wild card added to a natural canasta reduces it to a mixed canasta.

(c) As soon as a canasta is completed it must be squared up in a pile, with a natural red card on top if it is a natural canasta, a natural black card on top if it is a mixed canasta. This pile may be spread and the cards examined until the player next after the one who completed the canasta has ended his turn by discarding. Thereafter the canasta must remain in a pile, not subject to inspection, until the play of the deal ends.

24. A player may at any time combine two or more complete melds, including no more than three wild cards, made by his side; but no card once melded may be withdrawn from the meld of which it is part. (There is no "trading" for a wild card.)

Minimum Count

25. Every card melded has a point value, as follows:

Each joker	50
Each deuce	20
Each ace	20
Each king, queen, jack, 10, 9, 8	10
Each 7, 6, 5, 4, and black 3	5

26. The first meld made by a side is its initial meld. The initial meld must have a minimum count that depends upon the accumulated total score of that side at the beginning of the current deal, as follows:

TOTAL SCORE	MINIMUM COUNT
Minus	0
0 to 1,495	50
1,500 to 2,995	90
3,000 or more	120

27. For purposes of fulfilling the minimum count, a meld is valued by totalling the point values of all its component cards. A player may make two or more different melds in the same turn to achieve the minimum count. Bonuses do not count toward making the minimum except when a player goes out "concealed" (rule 49).

28. After a side has made its initial meld, either partner may make any valid melds without reference to any minimum count.

Taking the Discard Pile

29. The discard pile is frozen, as concerns a side, until that side has made its initial meld. The initial meld, whether made wholly from the hand or with help of the discard, unfreezes the pile for both partners, provided that it is not frozen additionally under rule 30.

30. Even for a side that has melded, the discard pile is frozen at any time that it contains a red trey (turned as up-card) or a wild card (up-card or a later discard). The pile remains frozen until it is taken up by some hand, whereupon the new pile commenced is not frozen unless a wild card is discarded (though it may be frozen for the opponents under rule 29).

31. At a time when the discard pile is frozen (for both sides or his side alone), a player may take the top card only to make a meld with two natural cards of the same rank from his hand.

32. At a time when the discard pile is not frozen, a player may draw the top card to make a meld with two cards from his hand, either two natural cards or one natural and one wild card, or to add to a meld of his side (see also rule 35).

33. In taking the discard, a player must proceed as follows (to show his legal right to it): face two cards from his hand that form a valid meld with the discard, under rule 31 or 32; lift off the top discard and place it with them; in the case of an initial meld, make such additional melds from his hand as are necessary to meet the minimum requirement. These additional melds may be separate from the first or added cards on the first. Next the player must take the rest of the discard pile into his hand, and he may then make all additional melds he chooses, with the aid of these cards; but these melds do not help to fulfill the minimum count.

34. The discard pile may not be taken when it is topped by a wild card or a black trey.

35. At a time when the pile is not frozen, a player may take the top card to add it to a previous meld of his side. (The card

may be added to a completed canasta, the same as to any other meld.) Correct procedure is to move the top card to such meld, then take the rest of the discard pile into the hand. But when the discard pile is only one card, and the player has only one card in his hand, he may not take it and go out unless he is forced to do so—see the next rule. (But in no case may a player go out when his side has not made a canasta and he cannot make one.)

Forcing

36. After the last card of the stock is drawn, play continues so long as each player in turn legally takes and melds the card discarded by his right-hand opponent. It is compulsory (when the stock is exhausted) to take the discard if it is legally possible to add it to a meld. (Making a discard that the next player must take, at this time, is called forcing.) The play ends when the player in turn does not take the discard, either because he cannot legally, or because he does not choose to. (A player is not forced to take a discard to meld it with cards from his hand.)

Going Out

37. A player goes out when he (legally) gets rid of the last card of his hand, either by discard or by meld.

38. A player may go out only if his side has melded at least one canasta (in two-hand play, two canastas). Failing this requirement, he must keep at least one card in his hand.

39. A player need not make a discard after going out; he may meld all of his remaining cards.

40. (a) If able to go out before drawing, or after drawing from the stock, a player may ask his partner "May I go out?" The partner must answer "Yes" or "No" and the player is bound by the reply.

(b) Permission to go out may not be asked by a player out of turn, nor when he has melded any card in that turn. (A player may go out without asking permission.)

(c) Having received the answer "No," the player who asked may take the discard pile if legally able to do so.

41. When any player goes out, play ends and the deal is scored.

Scoring a Deal

42. The side that goes out determines its net score for the deal as follows:

(a) Total the point values of the cards in its melds (rule 25).

(b) Total all bonuses under this schedule:

For going out	100
For each red trey (see rule 13)	200 or 100
For each natural canasta	500
For each mixed canasta	300
For concealed hand (see rules 48-50)	100

(c) Total the point values of all cards left in the hand of the player whose partner went out.

(d) Subtract item (c) from the sum of items (a) and (b).

43. The opponents of the side that went out determine their net score for the deal as prescribed under rule 42, with these differences: They cannot score for going out or for concealed hand; if this side has made no meld, the value of its red treys is deducted instead of added; point values of cards left in both hands are deducted.

44. If the last card of the stock is a red trey, the player drawing it may not discard; and after he has had an opportunity to meld, play ends. Play also ends when the stock is exhausted and the player whose turn it is fails to take the top discard. In either case the net scores are determined under rules 42 and 43, except that there can be no scores for going out and for concealed hand.

Scoring a Game

45. A game is won by the first side to reach a total of 5,000 points or more. If both sides reach 5,000 in the same deal (the

final deal is played out, even though it is known that one side will reach 5,000 after play ends), the side with the higher total wins.

46. There is no bonus for winning a game. Settlement is made on the difference of the final scores, which are the totals of the net deal scores.

47. The score should be recorded on paper, with one column for each side, and the record should show each net deal score together with the cumulative total of such scores for each side. (Minimum count for the initial meld on the next deal is fixed by this cumulative total.)

Concealed Hand

48. A player goes out with a concealed hand if he melds all his cards in one turn, having previously melded not a single card. (In going out concealed he may not add a card to a meld of his partner's.)

49. The player going out with a concealed hand must himself meld a complete canasta, but need not have any specific minimum count for an initial meld.

50. For concealed hand, a side scores a bonus of 100, additional to the bonus of 100 for going out.

IRREGULARITIES

Condonement

51. Any other rule to the contrary notwithstanding, there is no penalty for an irregularity if attention is not called to it before the next player in turn draws, melds, discards, or asks permission to go out; and—

(a) An insufficient initial meld, provided it is valid except for the minimum count, stands as a sufficient initial meld;

(b) Cards illegally exposed, in an invalid meld or on the table, are restored to the offender's hand;

(c) A draw or discard of two or more cards stands as regular, and the topmost card of the discard pile is the only discard available to the next player in turn;

(d) Cards illegally taken from the discard pile remain the property of the offender and remain part of his hand or of a valid meld, as the case may be.

New Deal

52. There must be a new deal:

(a) If it is ascertained, before the deal is completed, that the deck was not properly shuffled, cut, or dealt, or that a card is faced in dealing or in the deck.

(b) If it is ascertained, before each player has had a turn to play, that a player was dealt an incorrect number of cards, or that the deck contains an incorrect number or assortment of cards.

If attention is called to the irregularity within the time limit prescribed, the deal stands and play continues. An incorrect hand must be corrected as provided in rule 54. A card missing from the deck, if found, must be shown and then laid aside until the next deal; a foreign card is laid aside, and if it was in a player's hand he replaces it from the top of the stock.

Deal Out of Turn

53. If the wrong player deals, the deal stands; but if attention is called to it in time, the first play is made by the player whose turn it would have been, and he deals next.

Incorrect Hand

54. If a player has too many or too few cards—because he was dealt an incorrect hand, or drew more than one card, or failed to draw, and it is too late for rectification—

(a) With too many cards, he must discard without drawing

in each turn until his hand is correct, and he may not meld in any turn he began with too many cards;

(b) With too few cards, he plays on without correcting the error and without penalty.

55. If a player discards without drawing, he may be required to take the top card of the stock if attention is called to the irregularity before the next player has drawn.

Illegal Draw

56. (a) When a player touches the top card of the stock, or touches the discard pile, unless for the announced or apparent purpose of arranging the cards, he must draw from the pile touched.

(b) If the player directly or indirectly draws the top discard and cannot legally meld it, he must restore it and draw from the stock and 50 points are deducted from the score of his side.

(c) If, having indicated that he would draw from either the stock or the discard pile, a player attempts to draw from the other pile, the attempted change is void and 50 points are deducted from the score of his side; except that if the offender has already added any drawn card to his hand, rule 58 applies.

57. If in drawing from the stock a player sees any card he is not entitled to see, he must show such card to every player and restore it to the top of the stock. The player in turn after him may shuffle the stock before drawing, rather than draw a card so exposed; or may draw the top card of the stock.

58. (a) If a player draws and adds to his hand more than one card from the stock, rule 54(a) applies.

(b) If a player mixes any card from the discard pile with his hand without having legally melded the top card, he exposes his entire hand; the discard pile is reconstructed to the satisfaction of the offender's opponents; the offender must draw the top card of the stock; 200 points are deducted from the offender's score; and, in partnership play, all the offender's cards become penalty cards. But there is no penalty if the offender has previously shown cards from his hand that entitle him to take the top discard, or if the top discard can be added to a previous meld of the offender's side, and if the offender's opponents are satisfied that this is so.

Draw Out of Turn

59. If a player draws from the stock before the preceding player has discarded,

(a) if that player has already drawn, there is no penalty, but the offender may not change his draw when his turn comes.

(b) if that player has not drawn, 200 points are deducted from the offender's score if he has added the card to his hand; 100 points are deducted and he must restore the card if he has not added it to his hand.

60. If a player draws the top discard when it is not his turn, 100 points are deducted from his score, he must restore the card illegally drawn and must draw from the stock in his next turn, and in partnership play any cards he exposed to match the card illegally drawn become penalty cards. (Rule 58(b) may apply.)

Insufficient Meld

61. If for the initial meld of his side a player shows less than the required count, he may validate his meld if possible by rearrangement and with additional cards from his hand. If he does not do so before discarding, in partnership play each card exposed by him becomes a penalty card; in two-hand play, each card so exposed must be restored to his hand. (Section 56(b) may apply if he drew the top discard.)

Illegal Meld

62. If a player—

(a) makes a meld that includes more than three wild cards, but was not a completed canasta prior to his adding the fourth wild card;

(b) makes a meld that does not include at least two natural cards;
(c) makes a meld that does not include at least three cards;
(d) melds his last card when his side has not completed a canasta;
(e) melds his last card when he has asked permission to go out and his partner has answered "No";
(f) melds out by taking a one-card discard pile when he has only one card, but when there are one or more cards in the stock;

—he must on demand, before the next opponent in turn has drawn, validate his meld if legally possible, or retract any meld that cannot be validated; and in partnership play, any card he has exposed and cannot legally meld becomes a penalty card.

Meld Out of Turn

63. If a player melds when it is another player's turn to play, he must leave the cards melded on the table and meld them, if legally possible, when his turn to play comes; and—

(a) if it was an opponent's turn to play, 100 points are deducted from the offender's score;

(b) if it was the offender's partner's turn to play, 200 points are deducted from the offender's score—

and in partnership play, any card exposed by the offender that cannot be legally melded when his turn comes becomes a penalty card.

Penalty Points

64. (a) Any points to be deducted from an offender's score, in payment of a penalty, in partnership play apply in full to the score of the partnership.

(b) Penalty points do not affect the minimum initial meld, which depends solely on the score of each side at the beginning of the deal.

Exposed Cards—Penalty Cards

65. There is no penalty for illegal card exposure in two-hand or three-hand play in which each contestant plays for himself and has no partner, and in such play there are no penalty cards as defined in rule 67.

66. If a player simultaneously discards more than one card, he may elect the one that is his discard and retract the other(s). In partnership play, any card so retracted becomes a penalty card; in two- or three-hand play, such card is restored to the offender's hand. If the opponent next to play has drawn any such discard before attention is drawn to the irregularity, the other card(s) must be retracted.

67. (a) In partnership play, any card that a player illegally exposes on the table, or holds so that his partner may see its face, or indicates that he holds, by word or gesture, and any card designated by these rules to be a penalty card, becomes a penalty card.

(b) A penalty card must be left face up on the table, and the holder of such card must either meld it legally or discard it in each successive turn. If a player has more than one penalty card, he may choose which to discard.

(c) If, having a penalty card, a player discards from his hand, either opponent may either let the discard stand or require the discard of a previous penalty card and in the latter case the card discarded from the hand becomes a penalty card.

(d) A penalty card is treated as a card in the player's hand when the play of the deal ends.

Failure to Declare Red Trey

68. (a) If a player is dealt or draws a red trey, and fails to declare it before the play of the deal ends (provided he has had at least one turn to play), 500 points are deducted from the offender's score.

(b) If another player goes out before a player has had his first turn to play, he may face each red trey he holds and replace it by drawing from the stock.

Irregularities After Asking Permission to Go Out (Partnership Play Only)

69. (a) If a player asks permission to go out and does not do so, after receiving the answer "Yes"; or attempts to withdraw his question; or if the form of the question or of the partner's answer is otherwise than required by rule 40, and any additional information or advice is transmitted thereby; or if the player who asks shows any card or makes any meld before receiving his partner's answer; or if, having received the answer "No," the player who asks melds all his cards; either opponent may require the player who asked to go out, or not to go out.

(b) The opponents may not consult on the application of their rights as provided in rule 69(a), and if they attempt to do so they lose the right to decide whether or not the player shall go out.

70. If a player asks permission to go out and cannot do so after receiving the answer "Yes," or after an opponent requires him to go out as permitted by rule 69, 100 points are deducted from the score of his side.

71. If a player melds all his cards after asking permission to go out and receiving the answer "No," or if an opponent requires him not to go out as permitted by rule 69, he must rearrange his melds so as to leave at least one card in his hand; and any unmelded card in his hand becomes a penalty card.

Illegal Looking at Cards

72. If a player looks at previous discards, he is deemed to have drawn the top discard. Rule 56(b) or 60 may apply.

VARIATIONS IN CANASTA LAWS

Two-hand Canasta

There are four principal variations from the form of two-hand Canasta as played under the standard laws. These are:

Fifteen cards dealt to each player, but only one canasta required to go out.

Eleven cards dealt to each player, only one canasta required to go out.

Fifteen cards dealt to each player, two canastas required to go out, but at each turn each player draws *two* cards from the stock, discarding only one. A player who takes the pack, however, does not get an additional draw.

Fifteen cards dealt to each player, two canastas required to go out, but upon completion of the deal and before an up-card is turned each player looks at his hand and discards one card, immediately drawing a replacement card from the stock. Finally, the dealer turns the top card of the stock to be the usual up-card (and if this card is a red trey or wild card, it must be covered from the stock until the card so turned is not a red trey or wild card). This method assures that "the pack" will start off with no fewer than three cards.

Five-handed Canasta

With five players, Canasta is played as in four-hand with one player remaining out of action for each deal. The procedure is as follows:

Cut for partners; two high play against three low. The player with the lowest card remains out for the first deal. At the conclusion of that deal he replaces second-low, returning to active play at the conclusion of the second deal when he replaces the player who has not yet been out. Out players continue alternating until the conclusion of the game. To determine sides for the next game, all players may cut again, or the three players who have been alternating may cut among themselves to see which of their number shall join the previous side of two.

(It is advisable to decide in advance how the final score of each game is to be settled. Usually each player on the three-man side plays or collects the net point result of the game, the total being divided between the side of two. However, it is permissible for each player of the two-man side to pay or collect the net point result of the game, the total then being divided among the three. In any event, there is but one score for each team during the entire game, and the out-player participates in the result of all deals.)

Six-handed Canasta

Play is as in the four-handed game, except that the players divide themselves into two teams of three players each, the players of each team being seated alternately around the table.

When a player wishes to ask the question, "May I go out, partner?" he must address it specifically to either one of his partners and only that player may answer.

Three-pack Canasta

Six play, in three partnerships of two each; each player sits between two opponents, one of each other team:

```
          B     C
      A              A
          C     B
```

Three full packs and six jokers are shuffled together; back designs and colors need not be the same. Thirteen cards are dealt to each player. Game is 10,000, and when a side reaches 7,000 it needs 150 for its initial meld. Four red threes count only 100 each, but five threes count 1,000; all six count 1,200. A side needs two canastas to go out. The rules otherwise are as in four-hand Canasta.

The three-pack game may be played by any number of players from two to six.

MATHEMATICS OF CANASTA

Mathematical tables frighten most card players. Rows of cold figures seem unreal; it does not appear that they bear any relationship to the reality of actual play. But at times they can be a very helpful guide to the proper play in any specific circumstance.

For example, you can make the initial meld; this will increase the chance of your partner's getting the pack *if* he has at least one wild card. What are the chances?

TABLE I

You have no wild card. The chances that your partner was dealt one or more wild cards are:

    3 to 1   that he has at least one wild card
    2 to 3   that he has two or more wild cards
    9 to 1   that he has fewer than three wild cards

This calculation is based upon four-hand Canasta, in which each player is dealt eleven cards. It assumes also that you have seen no card dealt; but if you have seen your hand, and it contains no wild card, or no more than one wild card, the chances are not materially affected.

TABLE II

You are about to discard a single card from your hand. What is the chance that the opponent next to play has a pair of the same rank? a single card of the same rank, plus a wild card?

It is assumed that you can see twelve cards (your hand of eleven cards, in four-handed Canasta, plus the up-card), and that none of them is of the rank in question except the single card you propose to discard. However, if you have or can see another card of the same rank the chances are not materially affected.

It is:

4 to 1	that he does *not* have a pair of the same rank
3 to 2	that he *does* have a single card of the same rank
9 to 11	(slightly less than even) that he has a single card of the same rank plus a wild card

TABLE III

You have several places open to make a matched set, or to draw a particular card that will help your hand.

The following table gives your chance of drawing such a card in one or more draws. However, if the card needed is a joker, you have only one-half as much chance to get it (because there are only four jokers, as against eight cards of each other rank).

This table is not wholly accurate mathematically, because it assumes that you can see only twelve cards (your own eleven cards, in four-handed play, plus the up-card); but the chances are not materially affected by inconsequential cards exposed later, nor are they materially different when you hold more than eleven cards, as in two-handed Canasta.

The figures are expressed in percentages. That is, that fraction of 100 represented by the figure given; 98/100 means 98 chances out of 100, or 49 chances out of 50, which is to say 49 to 1 in favor of the contingency's occurring.

NUMBER OF DRAWS FROM THE STOCK	CHANCE OF DRAWING DESIRED CARD IF YOU HAVE THIS NUMBER OF PLACES OPEN:					
	1	2	3	4	5	6
1	1%	2%	3%	4%	5%	6%
2	2%	3%	6%	8%	10%	12%
3	3%	6%	9%	12%	15%	18%
4	4%	8%	12%	16%	20%	23%
5	5%	10%	15%	20%	24%	28%

GLOSSARY

Terms Used in Canasta

ADVERTISE—discard a card of same rank as a desired card, in the hope of inducing the opponent to discard the latter on the assumption it is safe.

BASE—A canasta base.

BASE COUNT or BASIC—the total of bonuses; all the score except the point value of cards.

BLIND DISCARD—one made without benefit of dead cards as a guide to safety.

BONUS—Any score other than the point value of the cards melded.

BREAK (a combination)—discard a card from a combination.

BUY—same as *draw*.

CALLING (a card)—able to use (the card) to form a matched set.

CANASTA—A meld of seven cards of the same rank, or four or more natural cards of that rank plus the necessary number of wild cards.

CANASTA BASE—A meld containing four natural cards which may be built into a canasta.

COMBINATION—a group of two cards that will become a matched set by addition of one specific card; in Canasta, these cards must be a pair of natural cards of the same rank.

COME-ON—a discard made for advertising purposes.

CONCEALED HAND—One that goes out in one turn, having made no previous meld, and without adding a card to a meld of partner's.

COUNT—the point-values of cards included in a meld, especially an initial meld.

COUNT, MINIMUM—The requirement in point-values for a valid initial meld.

CRACK—discard a card wanted by the opponent next in turn to play; or (chiefly in two-handed Canasta) meld first.

DEAD CARD—one whose matching cards cannot be used in a meld, or drawn, because they have already been melded.

DECK—the discard pile, or pack.

DISCARD—put a card from a hand onto the discard pile; the card so discarded.

DISCARD PILE—The heap of cards discarded and not taken up.

DRAW—take a card into the hand from the stock, or a card so taken; also, by extension, the top card of the discard pile taken to include in a meld.

EXPOSED CARD—in partnership play only, a card that is accidentally dropped or so held that partner can see its face. (Such a card may become a *penalty card*.)

Glossary

FILL—draw a card that turns a combination into a matched set.

5-POINT CARD—a card of rank 4 to 7, and any ♠ 3 or ♣ 3 legally melded (which may be only on the turn on which the holder goes out).

FORCING—discarding a card that the next player, under the rules, must take up.

FREEZE (the pack)—discard a wild card.

FROZEN—condition of the discard pile when, under the rules, it may be taken up only by matching the top card with a natural pair of the same rank.

GO DOWN—meld; especially, make the initial meld for oneself or one's side.

GO OUT—end the play by melding the remainder of one's cards, or by melding all one's cards but one, which is discarded.

GROUP—a matched set.

HIGH CARD—any card of rank 8 to K, and (sometimes) an ace.

HIT—discard a card that the opponent next in turn to play can take.

INITIAL MELD—the first meld made in a deal by a player or side, conforming to the specifications set forth by the Canasta laws.

LAY DOWN—meld.

LAY OFF—add a suitable card to a meld of one's side or oneself.

LOW CARD—any card of rank 4 to 7, and any ♠ 3 or ♣ 3 if melded in the turn in which one goes out.

MATCHED CARD—one that is part of a matched set.

MATCHED SET—three or more cards which, under the rules, may be melded together; in Canasta, three or more cards of the same rank, under the rules.

MELD—a matched set; to place a matched set on the table; to lay off.

MIXED CANASTA—A canasta including one or more wild cards.

NATURAL CANASTA—A canasta of seven or eight natural cards.

NATURAL CARD—any card but a joker, deuce, or three; a card that is not wild.

OFF CARD—one that does not make a matched set or combination.

PACK—the discard pile.

PLAYER—a card that can be added to a meld.

PRIZE PILE—a discard pile that is frozen.

PURE CANASTA—A natural canasta.

REDUCE—discard a card or cards to reduce the count of cards in one's hand if an opponent goes out.

RUN—a sequence (not valid in Canasta).

SAFE—said of a discard that cannot be taken by the opponent next in turn.

SEQUENCE—three or more cards of the same suit in sequence (not valid in Canasta).

SET—matched set; also a position where a player is within one card of being able to go out.

SHED—discard.

SPLIT—discard a card from a combination.

STOCK—the remainder of the pack after the original hands are dealt.

STOP-CARD — A discard which may not be taken up by the next player; specifically, a black trey or wild card.

TAKE UP—draw from the discard pile.

10-POINT CARD—any card of rank 8 to K.

TENTH CARD—a card counting 10 points—in Canasta, a card of rank 8 to K. [This term is seldom used in Canasta.]

TRIO—three natural cards of the same rank.

TRIPLET—three natural cards of the same rank; same as trio.

UNLOAD—discard or meld cards so as to reduce the count of cards in one's hand if another player goes out.

UP-CARD—the first card turned face up from the stock, to start the discard pile.

WILD CARD—one that may be designated by the holder to be of any rank.

WILD DISCARD—one that, so far as the discarder knows, can be taken up by the opponent next to play.